COMPLETE
LIGHTING DESIGN

QUARRY

A Practical Design Guide
for Perfect Lighting

COMPLETE
LIGHTING DESIGN

GLOUCESTER MASSACHUSETTS

QUARRY
BOOKS

Marilyn Zelinsky-Syarto

First published in the United States of America by
Quarry Books, a member of
Quayside Publishing Group
33 Commercial Street
Gloucester, Massachusetts 01930-5089
Telephone: (978) 282-9590
Fax: (978) 283-2742
www.rockpub.com

Library of Congress Cataloging-in-Publication Data
Zelinsky, Marilyn.
    Complete lighting design : a practical design guide for
perfect lighting / Marilyn Zelinsky
    Syarto.
        p. cm.
    ISBN 1-59253-247-0 (pbk.)
    1. Lighting, Architectural and decorative. I. Title.
NK2115.5.L5Z45 2006
    729'.28—dc22   2006002722
                                                    CIP

ISBN 1-59253-247-0

10 9 8 7 6 5 4 3 2 1

Design: Rockport Publishers
Layout: Dutton & Sherman
Cover image: Björg Magnea/Igloo Design Group
Back cover images: Courtesy of DMAC Architecture (left);
Courtesy of Verbeck Design Studios, Inc. (middle); Douglas
Hope Hooper/Avalon Artistic Landscape Lighting (right)

Printed in Singapore

CONTENTS

Introduction 009

SECTION ONE: PLANNING PERFECT LIGHTING 011

Principles and Planning 012
IN FOCUS: UNDERSTANDING DAYLIGHT AND NIGHTTIME LIGHTING EFFECTS 013

LIGHTING FIXTURES 014
ARCHITECTURAL INTERIOR LUMINAIRES 014
SUSPENDED FIXTURES 016
RECESSED AND TRACK LIGHTING 018
BATH AND VANITY FIXTURES 019
SCONCES AND WALL FIXTURES 020
IN FOCUS: HOME THEATER LIGHTING 021

Portable lighting fixtures 022
TABLE LAMPS 022
IN FOCUS: LIGHTING EFFECTS FROM SHADES AND DIFFUSERS 023
FLOOR LAMPS 024
ACCENT LIGHT FIXTURES 025

Exterior Luminaires 026
ARCHITECTURAL LANDSCAPE LIGHTING 026

Portable Exterior fixtures 028
IN FOCUS: WHAT'S NEW IN SOLAR LIGHTING 029

Lamp and Bulb Gallery 030
IN FOCUS: MORE LIGHT, LESS MONEY 033
ANTIQUE AND VINTAGE BULBS 034

SECTION TWO: PROJECTS WITH LIGHTING DESIGNS AND IDEAS 037

Living and Dining Spaces 038
THE ART OF LIGHT 040
A CANOPY OF LIGHTED COVES 046
COUTURE LIGHTING 050
THE NEW FIREPLACE 054
THE SHELF LIFE OF LIGHT 056
PLANES OF LIGHT 058
VIGNETTES OF LIGHT 060
A LAYERING OF LOVELINESS 064
UNDERLIGHTING A LIVING SPACE 066
THE WONDER OF NATURE'S LIGHT 068
SLEEPING SPACES 070
BOXED BRILLIANCE 072
MOOD LIGHTING 076
A CRISP WHITE LIGHT 078
LIGHT DOCK 080

ILLUMINATING A RETREAT 084

CAPTURING DAYLIGHT 086

KITCHEN AND BATHS 088

A CHEF'S DELIGHT 090

A RADIANT REDWOOD BATH 092

A DESIGNER'S OWN LIGHTING PLAN 094

RENEWING A KITCHEN WITH LIGHT 096

THE PAMPERED KITCHEN AND BATH 098

IN FOCUS: A WELL-LIT CLOSET 101

STAIRS AND HALLS 102

A FLOATING STAIRWAY 104

THE LIGHT DOWN THE HALL 105

NIGHT LIGHT 106

WALLS OF LIGHT 107

LIGHTING A RICH, DARK SPACE 108

OUTDOOR SPACES 110

AN OPTICAL ILLUSION 112

AN OUTDOOR DESTINATION 114

IN FOCUS: AN ESSENTIAL LIGHTING TOOL 119

THE FLOW OF LIGHT 120

A PLAY OF LIGHT AND SHADOWS 122

A SUBTLE BEACON OF LIGHT 126

TECHNIQUES OF THE TRADE 128

COMPLETE DWELLINGS 132

STRETCHING SPACE WITH LIGHT 134

A HOUSE WITH A LIGHT TOUCH 140

THE ICE BOX 146

BY THE LIGHT OF THE MOON 150

SHEETS OF LIGHT 156

A HOME BRIMMING WITH HEIRLOOM LIGHTS 162

GLOSSARY OF LIGHTING TERMS 168

CONTRIBUTING LIGHTING DESIGNERS, ARCHITECTS, AND INTERIOR DESIGNERS 171

MANUFACTURERS, SUPPLIERS, PRODUCTS, AND ONLINE RESOURCES 173

PHOTOGRAPHER CREDITS 175

ACKNOWLEDGMENTS 176

ABOUT THE AUTHOR 176

INTRODUCTION

Take a twilight tour of an upscale neighborhood, and no doubt you'll see homes that have that certain curb appeal and look so inviting, yet you can't pinpoint the concrete reason *why* they're so welcoming. You'll notice the glow, an elusive aura surrounding these homes that brings alive the landscape and interiors, especially as night begins to fall. Each outdoor space, garden, and tree looks full and lush. Looking in through the windows at night, when the interiors are on display, the rooms take on a romantic glow that beckons you inside. You'll wonder, "What's the secret to creating that kind of captivating atmosphere?" The secret is in the lighting.

When a house doesn't look right or feel comfortable, sometimes the heart of the problem is in the lighting. But, *why* is lighting so important? The right type of lighting provides myriad advantages while the wrong type of lighting may flaw the beauty of an otherwise perfect house and landscape design. Light can shape and accentuate objects or flatten them, unveil true colors or distort them, provide a lively environment or a gloomy one, produce glare that causes discomfort, or be placed in a way that reduces brightness and increases visibility. The way a home and landscape is lit—inside and out—prepares visitors for the experience they perceive they'll have once inside the house. If the experience of walking up to a house is enjoyable, visitors are more likely to feel good about the home when they go inside. A house that's well lit exudes comfort and warmth and gives guests a calming feeling that once they are inside, they will be well taken care of.

But when we sense a problem with our home, lighting is rarely the first thing that we think of needing to be fixed, upgraded, or appropriately designed. Perhaps we buy a higher wattage bulb to brighten a room, or upgrade a shade or two, and randomly place path lighting so you can see where you are going at night. Yet, we still might get dismal results. Instead, we try to fix everything else about the house, or even move because we cannot tolerate the way the house looks and feels rather than deal with the lighting issue.

It's easier said than done to properly light your home. An average size room needs four to five different light sources. The decision process, and enormous variety of products, can make anyone's head spin. The incandescent light bulb—the beloved

bulb we're used to—now has many new competitors: from a new generation of fluorescent bulbs to halogen to new LED bulbs. Then, there are the many and common questions—will compact fluorescent bulbs fit into standard fixtures that typically take standard incandescent bulbs? What is the difference between a MR-11 and a MR-15 lamp? What shape bulb—globe, candelabra, flame shape, or cone shape—is best for which fixture? What fixtures and bulbs are best for interior and exterior wet areas? What's the difference between solar and low voltage path lighting? Can concealed lighting retrofit into my home's design?

Lighting has come a long way since candles and oil-burning lamps were the main sources of light prior to the 1800s. From the gas lamps of the early 1800s to the electric arc lamps that made their way into homes by the mid 1800s, it was the early rendition of the incandescent bulb, successfully developed by inventor Thomas Edison in 1879, that marked the birth of electric lighting and the electric age. By 1910, with the development of tungsten filament bulbs, the electric light superceded all other forms of lighting. From there, we saw the advent of fluorescent light popularized in commercial spaces between 1939 and 1950. The science and art of lighting continues to progress. Today, architects and designers rely on the expertise of lighting designers to integrate this technical and functional aspect of architecture into the design of a space.

As you'll see in the projects included in this book, there are an infinite number of ways to create beautiful lighting—from choosing the correct fixture to highlight artwork, properly illuminating an outdoor entryway, or finding out where to buy the right antique light bulb. This book is divided into three sections and organized to be a useful resource as well as an inspiration and idea generator. It will help guide you in designing your own lighting plan. The first section is a sourcebook of every conceivable type of architectural and portable lighting fixture and lamp—along with tips to help you select which option is best for you. The second section showcases expert interior and exterior lighting projects—featuring every room and space—with lighting design plans and expert words of advice on how to make the ideas your own. The final section is a resource guide with phone numbers, contact information, and, if available, websites for every profession, service, and product in the book.

As you peruse this book, you'll see how lighting is more than just a complementary element; it's an essential part of a home's design that will complete and enhance each space to bring out its best features—the way the architect, designer, and homeowner intended each room to be.

The overall lighting concept of this contemporary home, designed by Marcus Gleysteen, Gleysteen Design, was to light surfaces and spaces both inside and out with as few visible sources as possible. The recessed lights in the exterior overhanging eaves light the space beyond the living room. The lighting scheme beckons guests indoors, and at the same time, creates a comforting haven on the deck.

SECTION ONE:
PLANNING PERFECT LIGHTING

INTERIOR FIXTURES, EXTERIOR FIXTURES, BULBS, AND MORE

"When lighting is done well, it will furnish a room," says Ann Videriksen, lighting designer and owner of Los Angeles-based Design Communication. But no one ever said that it would be easy to light a room, much less the entire interior and exterior of a home. But analyzing and knowing the pros and cons of each of your rooms and exterior spaces will help organize an efficient and aesthetically graceful lighting plan. Lighting can be used to transform a space *if* you have a sense of what you'd like to transform and achieve through the use of light. Whether it's an entire lighting plan for the house, or a relatively inexpensive fixture upgrade for one room, lighting gives you the tools to update, brighten, and bring out the best features of your house.

The first section of the book summarizes the basic principles and planning techniques of lighting, and then lets you delve into the vast world of fixtures and bulbs for indoor and outdoor use. Such recent trends as LED lights, pendant lights, the streamlined track lighting designs, and expansive trim and housing options in today's recessed interior lighting fixtures are discussed, as well as the strides made in solar lighting for outdoor use.

Finding favorite lighting designs is not as easy as clipping pictures and images from shelter magazines and design books. The effects of lighting are so much more intangible than the effects of other products. When you're planning your lighting scheme, the key is to get out and visit as many lighting stores and lighting showrooms as possible. In addition, it's always a good idea to visit model homes in your area to see what's new for lighting high ceilings, angled walls, small spaces, large spaces, foyers, and landscapes.

What will help is if you take one room at a time and figure out two levels of information. First, what do you want the overall feeling of the room to be—energetic, romantic, calm, or task-oriented? Secondly, determine more specifically what you need to accomplish in each of those rooms (reading, working, cooking, sewing, entertaining, etc.). Armed with each room's profile, you are ready to take on the lighting world (ideally with the help of a lighting specialist).

Outdoor lighting requires much of the same line of questioning. Underlighting and overlighting yards remain two of the biggest mistakes homeowners make with landscape lighting. Rather than turning shadowy paths into inviting walkways, we put solar lights where low-voltage or line-voltage lights should go, and we suffer when we can't see the sidewalk clearly at night. Or the way we place our spotlights make the beautiful tree with the statuesque branches in the front yard take on a more haunting look when its startling shadow looks more like a Halloween movie prop than a graceful silhouette against the sky. Do your best to draw your property (including the house), mark the paths, the dark spots, play and entertaining areas, and the special elements that you'd like to highlight. Once you've mapped it out, take the drawing with you every time you venture out to a lighting store and by all means use it while consulting with lighting specialists.

Schoolhouse Electric's vintage-style fixtures with hand-blown glass shades have become fashionable for their unique look that fits into both restored homes as well as contemporary dwellings.

PRINCIPLES AND PLANNING

Lighting has a physical and psychological effect on most people. It is not presumptuous to say that the light our eyes see governs our personal view of the world. That's how powerful light can be. Not only can a room with poor lighting become boring, more importantly, it's fatiguing for us to be in a room with the wrong lighting. That's why it's important to understand the fundamental principles behind the types of lighting.

LAYERED LIGHTING—PRINCIPLE #1
Rooms with only overhead lighting give off a dull tinge to the colors in the space. That's because the light becomes overly diffused and does not bring focus or brilliance to any one object. In most rooms, it takes a handful of different types of fixtures to create an appropriate lighting plan. To achieve this, it's best to layer—or combine—three basic types of lighting.

Ambient lighting, often from overhead fixtures, sometimes from concealed fixtures (such as in cove and tray ceilings), fills an entire space with diffused light.

Task lighting, often in the form of a table lamp, bathroom mirror lights, or under-counter kitchen lights, provides a direct beam of light that allows you to do specific activities, such as reading or putting on makeup, with efficiency.

Accent lighting has many forms, including recessed spotlights, wall washers, wand and track lighting, concealed fixtures (such as cove and toe-kick lighting), in- and under-cabinet lighting, and decorative portable lamps. Accent lights add interest or highlight an object, artwork, or an unusual architectural feature in a room.

MANIPULATING SPACE—PRINCIPLE #2
To make small spaces larger, limit the amount of objects or surfaces that are accent lit, and instead, focus on ambient lighting. When you reduce the amount of accent lighting in a room and rely more on ambient lighting, you'll create the appearance of a larger space. That's because you're reducing the number of surfaces highlighted by light. When surfaces recede, a space feels larger. Another tip from designers: If a room has a low ceiling, uplights will direct light up and "push" up the horizontal plane, making it feel taller. Designers make hot rooms feel cooler with light, as well. In hot climates, lighting is often used to create a physiologically-induced, cooled-down ambience. By concealing the lighting or placing it high above furnishings or people's heads, and using sconces to bounce light off

of light-colored walls and ceilings, the space won't feel stifling to the senses. Lighting can make a cold room feel warmer if the source produces a yellow-white light. A yellow-white cast of light reflected off light-colored surfaces gives the eye a perception of warm, relaxed ambient light.

COLOR EFFECTS—PRINCIPLE #3
The type of lighting you use in a room greatly affects the way you perceive color in the space. Lighting can subdue color or make it pop. To subdue color in a room, use floor lamps and scones that are uplights. The beam of light will focus on the ceiling, not on the surrounding colors and textures. To strengthen color in a room, the use of sconces and wall fixtures that are not uplights will intensify colors because light beams reflect and bounce off horizontal surfaces to highlight neighboring tones. Consider that dark-colored rooms require twice as much light (in terms of fixtures and wattage) as light-colored rooms. Dark ceilings, walls, and other surfaces absorb four times as much light as light-colored surfaces.

PLANNING FOR VOLTAGE VARIATIONS
Using the wrong voltage for the wrong application will harm the lights and the electrical system of your home. Voltage differences are especially worth noting between American and European fixtures. Since most plugs in the United States are 120V and most in Europe operate on 220V, there's an obvious obstacle if you plan on installing a beautiful Italian line-voltage fixture in your dining room. Since a European plug won't fit into an American plug, a converter will be necessary, but only in a 220V circuit. American fixtures fizzle out when plugged into a European outlet.

It's best to remember the basics: Line-voltage lights work with the standard voltage found in electric junction boxes and outlets, such as 120V in the United States and 220V in Europe.

Outdoor lighting poses another voltage issue. According to landscape lighting designers, voltage drops can be severe with low-voltage systems, and that will impede performance of the best lighting plan. "There are three elements which must be considered when dealing with this issue—cable size (gauge), wattage load, and total distance (lineal feet) of cable from the transformer to the fixture," warns Mark Carlson of Avalon Artistic Landscape Lighting. Whether it's indoor or outdoor lighting, now is the time to venture out to a lighting supply store and converse with the professionals.

IN FOCUS:

UNDERSTANDING DAYLIGHT AND NIGHTTIME LIGHT EFFECTS

The fourth type of lighting isn't artificial. It's daylight. An interior or exterior space appears different when washed in daylight than it does when it's illuminated by artificial light. Most of us under- or overlight a space during the daytime and the nighttime, doing injustice to the color, architectural elements, and comfort we will experience in the room.

During the daytime, it's important to let in as much natural light as possible. That's because we need day-light—or natural light—to adequately stimulate our brains and biological functions. The blue color of the sky, greens of vegetation, and earth tones are part of our natural environment. Environments that simulate these conditions make us feel most comfortable and relaxed. Incandescent and cool white fluorescent lamps do not provide the effects of daylight. Full-spectrum fluorescent illumination provides this simulation although the light levels are much lower than that of daylight.

However, there is the question of what *kind* of daylight do you want in your house? Most of us just shrug our shoulders and say we want plain old daylight. "However, this raises an interesting point," says lighting designer Mark Kubicki, who lives and works in New York City. "When clients ask for natural daylight, what kind of daylight they are asking for needs to be clarified. Is it that light in the middle of a summer or a winter day, or is it the light they experienced in Denmark or Cuba, on a sunny day or a cloudy one, in an open field or the dappled light under a tall oak tree? They are all very different interpretations of the same light, and just as beautiful, but interiors will look different in each light." Kubicki says that he notices a dif-ference in the autumn time when he senses a "flatness" of the light in New York City, whereas at the same time during the year, the light in New England would be more golden.

Architect Kar-Hwa Ho explains how different daylights work in an interior. He agrees with Kubicki that lat-itude and immediate surroundings affect the quality of light and how we perceive the objects around us. "One only has to look at Dutch still life paintings, Venetian, or Scandinavian landscapes to appreciate the different effect light has on a particular environment." He goes on to explain: "The perceived object takes on the cast of that reflected light. Typically, northern light is even and 'cooler' because it is reflected off the sky dome while southern light, because it is direct, is 'warmer' with more glare and hot spots."

ROOM WITH A VIEW

The daytime view out the window of the reading nook is a clear shot of the trees. At night, though, improper lighting would make the view outside the window a black hole. Here, lighting designer Janet Lennox Moyer subtly lights the trees with down-lights set under the home's eaves. But the view to the outside has more to do with the careful, yet simple, planning of the interior lighting. "Controlling the interior light in the nook allows the homeowner to see out through the window at night to enjoy the structure of the trees," says Moyer. "Having the visual connection to the exterior helps us enjoy our landscapes at night, but, also makes interior spaces feel larger." In addition, recessed adjustable fixtures in the nook are aimed to highlight the art and to allow some light to spill onto the seating area at night just where someone would be holding their book for reading.

LIGHTING FIXTURES

ARCHITECTURAL INTERIOR LUMINAIRES

Increasing appetites for new home construction and home renovations influence fixture manufacturers to design more exciting and provocative architectural lighting fixtures. Larger homes require more architectural lighting—or luminaires that are permanently installed and planned for in the lighting or wiring plan of a home. Lighting trends change slowly—the fixture bought today will last in style and durability for 5 to 10 years or longer. However, manufacturers continuously respond to consumers' desire for color and novel materials. Recent trends point to the demand for oversized foyer pieces for dramatic, grand entryways, mini-chandeliers for powder rooms, bedrooms, hallways, and other small spaces, and colorful pendants for kitchen applications.

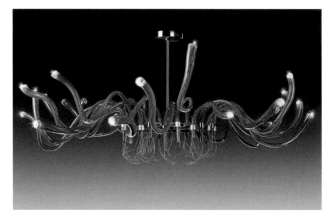

DINING TABLE CHANDELIER
The golden rule in choosing a dining room table chandelier is that its diameter should be equal to half the width of the table. That means a typical table width of 54 inches (137 cm) would require a chandelier with a 27 inch (69 cm) diameter. With extra long tables expanding six feet (1.8 m) plus, it's challenging to find a fixture in just the right scale. This 43 inch (109 cm) -long, eight-light fixture from Hubbardton Forge is engineered to fit elegantly above an elongated table. The shape of the fixture is oval rather than round in order to illuminate more dining space, and the arms have friction swivel for alignment over any shape of table.

CONTEMPORARY CHANDELIER
The popular ornate look of chandeliers waned in the 1990s, but the fixture has made a comeback in traditional or contemporary style. The materials, shapes, color, and light sources of today's chandeliers can dramatically differ from the classic crystal or wrought iron version. This brightly colored contemporary chandelier from Leucos has small halogen lamps embedded in the end of each serpentinelike Venetian glass arm.

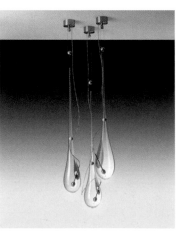

LEFT: MINI-CHANDELIER
Chandeliers are no longer relegated only to dining areas and foyers. Some sizes, designs, and finishes are delicate enough to hang in powder rooms and bedrooms. Laura Ashley's romantic and diminutive Lavenham model, an eight-light chandelier with cut-glass droplets and candle-style light fittings with a soft cream finish, fits into any bath or bedroom.

RIGHT: CABLE PENDANT
One recent trend is to group two or more pendants together as a way to bring focus to a surface such as a dining table or kitchen island. This Venetian glass pendant from Leucos is suspended from a height-adjustable cable, allowing for multiple units to be hung at varying heights. The effect is that of drops of water suspended in air, and the enclosed halogen lamp emits a glow from within.

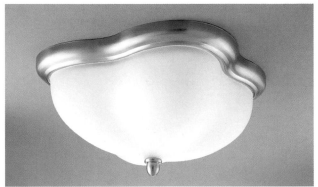

FLUSH CEILING MOUNT

For years, ceiling mounted fixtures came in a basic domed shape in smooth white glass meant only to cover bare bulbs. Though many of the standard designs still remain popular, this once-forgotten fixture now comes in new designs, materials, and colors meant to make better use of a room's fifth wall. Ballard's Mosaic Tile ceiling mount fixture casts a halo of light onto the ceiling through the handset glass tiles.

SEMI-FLUSH CEILING MOUNT

As with a flush-mount fixture, the semi-flush mount fixture is meant to throw off general or ambient light to an area from above eye level. However, a semi-flush mount hangs slightly lower than a flush mount, entrapping the light to allow more of it to bounce up onto the ceiling. If it's well designed like Michael Grave's etched opal glass shade and brushed nickel fixture created for Progress Lighting, then even a small ceiling fixture can become the focus of a room. This fixture is 11 inches (28 cm) high in comparison to its coordinating flush mount version, which is 7 1/2 inches (19 cm) high.

LEFT: SINGLE PENDANT DOWNLIGHT

A single pendant downlight is all that's necessary for soft light over a small table or to subtly highlight a corner of a room. This simple, slim fixture from Ikea has a mouth-blown double glass shade that takes a barely there 25-watt bulb. Though the shade is narrow, the glass lets the glow from the bulb project out from the sides, as well as down onto a surface.

RIGHT: MULTIPLE PENDANTS

Now that kitchen islands—small and large—are popular, there's an abundance of boldly designed multiple pendants in vibrant colors, such as this one from Leucos with its glossy orange glass diffuser. The most important point to consider when choosing a pendant is that the fixture will give off its light according to the diameter of its shade. The larger the shade, the subtler the light will be that is cast on the surface. The narrower the shade, the more pinpointed the light will be.

LEFT: FOYER CHANDELIER

The popularity of the two-story foyer with its vaulted ceiling and high, wide window means the entryway's light fixture becomes the main focus, even from the curb. The larger the space, the larger the chandelier, which makes installation a challenge. A wrought iron or crystal chandelier can come as large as 4-feet (1.2 m) tall and 4-feet (1.2 m) wide and weigh over 200 pounds (90.7 kilos), making it necessary to mount it to a beam to support the weight. More choices in size, weight, and materials are becoming available. This freshly styled chandelier from Tech Lighting, called Rhapsody, weighs a mere 16 pounds (7.3 kilos) because it's designed with flight paper shades over MR16 lamps. Flight paper, a decorative heat-resistant paper, is lightweight and brings an airy, contemporary look to a fixture.

RIGHT: MULTIPLE PENDANTS ON CANOPY

To keep specifications simple, there are multiple pendants that are designed to emerge from one canopy. This modern version in a brushed nickel finish from Rejuvenation has three pendants hanging at premeasured varying heights from a 12-inch (30 cm) -diameter canopy; the shortest pendant hangs down 12 inches (30 cm), the longest is 36 inches (91 cm).

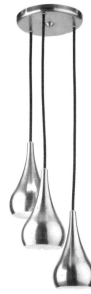

SUSPENDED FIXTURES

Suspended fixtures, many known as pendant lights, became popular in the 1970s when the advent of lightweight, moldable, and inexpensive heat-resistant plastics created a whole new category of lighting. In the years to come, lightweight blown glass-shaded pendant fixtures would be able to add even more color to any room in the house. Suspended fixtures dramatically change the look of a room since there are so many material and color choices, from a traditional bowl fixture over a dining room table to the new models of pot racks embedded with task lights for the kitchen preparation work surface. Suspended fixtures need to be used in a layered lighting scheme because they will not provide enough ambient light for an entire room.

It's important to determine the correct length to hang a pendant over a kitchen island. Some manufacturers suggest hanging a balloon attached to a string to help decide the best length. As a general rule, the bottom of a small single pendant should hang 36 inches (0.9 meter) above the surface. If it hangs too low it's an obstacle and only creates small pools of light onto the surface. A fixture that's too high with the bulb at eye level (whether seated or standing) creates an uncomfortable glare.

Ceiling fans with light kits are now counted among the choices in suspended fixtures. Though pendant lights and ceiling fans are both considered suspended fixtures, they illuminate a room differently. Lighted fans hang closer to the ceiling and provide ambient illumination in a room. Pendant fixtures hang lower and provide targeted task lighting (over a kitchen island work surface, for example).

KITCHEN ISLAND PENDANTS
Pendants are popular fixtures for kitchen islands. Oversized pendants, such as this Mission-style Crystal Springs three-light model from Rejuvenation, will provide some of the ambient lighting for the kitchen because it's meant to hang higher above the island than smaller fixtures. The plain, frosted, glass shades also help diffuse light around the counter rather than just downward.

KITCHEN POT RACK LIGHT
Another suspended fixture for a kitchen island is a pot rack with lighting to bring additional task illumination to the work surface. This rack, from Hubbardton Forge, has a mahogany finish and includes four glass tubes in a glossy dusk finish to cover the cans. MR-16 50-watt lensed bulbs illuminate the surface while making the hanging pots shine.

LEFT: FLOATING DIFFUSERS
Pendant diffusers come in all shapes and sizes. Artemide's Logico Mini Triple Suspended fixture has nested diffusers in hand-blown glass with a satin finish designed to appear like clouds above. The light from this pendant will filter out of the white glass diffusers to give a room a soft ambient illumination.

RIGHT: GLOBE PENDANT
Pendants can be simple and elegant, like this Hemisphere Pendant from Nessen Lighting and designed by Shelton, Mindel & Associates Architects. Its design is characterized by its hand-blown glass globe 15 inches (38 cm) in diameter, a top half that is clear glass, and a bottom half that is sandblasted white glass to obscure the light source—an incandescent bulb.

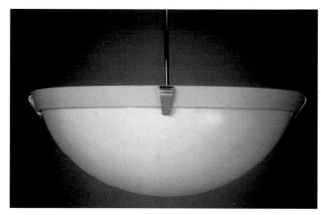

FORTUNY LAMPS

The fine fabrics of Mariano Fortuny, who lived from 1871 to 1949 in Venice, come to life on Fortuny Lamps available through retailers today. The eclectic Fortuny, who invented the dimmer switch, continued to experiment with newly invented electric light at the turn of the century. He translated his knowledge into embellished suspended lamps of silk that take on an oriental spirit. This version, Samarkanda Fortuny, available through Bellissimo, has an ornamental disk that rests on a pleated helmet of fabric.

SUSPENDED UPLIGHT

Suspended uplights have bowl-shaped shades that cast light upward for an even glow on the ceiling, and give off a soft, diffused light down into the space. A bowl pendant, like this Imperial Bowl Pendant from Lam Lighting, is a classic shape used in entryways, over dining tables, and even in powder rooms. If hanging a bowl fixture over a dining room table, the general rule for average height ceilings is to hang it 30 inches (76 cm) above the surface.

LEFT: PENDANT FOR LARGE ROOM

Large pendant fixtures will offer enough ambient light for a room. This sizeable pendant, Scala from Luxo, is meant to illuminate large foyers. Its white-coated, steel louvers eliminate glare and hide the compact fluorescent bulb light source while releasing a comfortable light.

RIGHT: CABLE SUSPENDED FIXTURE

A hanging fixture that uses a cable immediately brings a contemporary look to a space. The Tian Xia Meta fixture from Artemide hangs from three cables and brings new technology to a homeowner's fingertips. A microprocessor and infrared receiver housed inside the canopy controls the lighting created by three halogen lamps with colored lenses. Another white halogen bulb illuminates the ceiling, and the light show is directed by remote control.

FLUSH CEILING FAN WITH LIGHT

This fan, the Aurora Hugger from The Modern Fan Company, is designed for a room with a low ceiling, common among mid-century homes, such as ranch-style dwellings. Though it is a suspended fixture, it will provide enough ambient lighting for a small- to medium-sized room. The fixture is also suitable for damp locations, making it ideal for existing homes.

SUSPENDED CEILING FAN WITH LIGHT

The suspended ceiling fan hangs 18 inches (46 cm) to 24 inches (61 cm) from the ceiling. Halo, from The Modern Fan Company, integrates the fan function with a light that takes a 26W CFL or a 100-watt incandescent bulb. The glowing amber glass diffuser tones down the cool white of a fluorescent bulb while the opal white glass diffuser creates a focused downward light.

RECESSED AND TRACK LIGHTING

Recessed lighting, the basic workhorse light fixture seen mostly in renovated basements years ago, has experienced a renaissance. In the past, recessed lighting consisted of a 120-watt incandescent bulb hanging straight down inside a trimmed can mounted in the ceiling. Today's recessed lighting fixture still has clean lines, but might have a halogen bulb set at an angle in an eyeball fixture for a concentrated and sparkling beam of light. Today's streamlined track lighting designs still offer all the advantages of older versions. Track lighting brings flexibility to a room, and it is best used on sloped ceilings since most recessed fixtures can't be aimed on a piece of artwork on an adjacent wall.

LEFT: CABLE HUNG PENDANTS
Track lighting combines with pendant lighting to create a fresh, modern look. Brilliantly colored, glass pendants hang on Tech Lighting's T~trak™ in front of a fireplace in a room with high ceilings.

RIGHT: CURVED TRACK LIGHTING
The curved low-voltage cable lighting system that illuminates this hallway, designed by architect Laurence "Renzo" Verbeck of Verbeck Design Group, was used as a playful gesture contrasting the more rectilinear elements in the upper hallway and gallery. The cherry wood ceiling paneling draws the eye through the length of the space, while the fixture curves playfully in and out of the art niches to invite exploration. MR-16 halogen lamps bring out the artworks' vivid color, and they have great beam variability. A fixture such as this can be found at Tech Lighting. The manufacturer's MonoRail model is hand-bendable to custom-create configurations for any size space.

TUBULAR SKYLIGHT
The bright spots of light in this bathroom (left) and home office (right) may look like recessed fixtures, but they are actually tubular skylights that capture sunlight from the roof and redirect it down a highly reflective shaft. The Solatube skylight works well in a lighting scheme with other recessed lighting fixtures because of its round design.

RECESSED CEILING WALL WASHER
The sturdy, lightweight, 22-gauge, cold-rolled steel housing of this recessed downlight is used for interior and exterior applications where a high-lumen output through a thin 8- or 9-inch (20 cm or 23 cm) -aperture for wall washing is desired. The Architekture housing (left), from Prescolite, takes CFLs for higher energy efficiency. Prescolite's Signos-6 collection (right) of decorative, architectural-inspired, lattice glass and frosted-glass trim, fits over the opening of each downlight.

TRACK FIXTURES WITHOUT TRACK
Some spaces call for track lighting, but installing a long track would look awkward or would be problematic. For those instances, Edison Price Lighting created a short track lighting system, called Unicep. The Unicep R (left) recesses into gypsum board ceilings and is a track long enough and discreet enough to accept one wand track light fixture. (There is also a version that recesses into plaster and wood ceilings.) The rounded Unicep S model (right) mounts onto an outlet box on a ceiling, and again accepts one wand track light fixture.

BATH AND VANITY FIXTURES

The most important light in a bath is the one around the mirror. Avoid using a single downlight in the ceiling over the sink area. "It causes the 'racoon effect' with heavily shadowing of the eye sockets and other contours of the face," says Brian Hart, general manager of Forecast Lighting, a division of Lightolier. "The best way to light the face is to flank each side of the face with sconces on the wall, as well as the light above to highlight the hair and provide a general illumination effect."

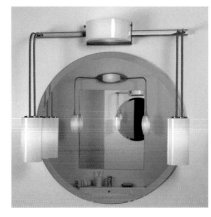

SHADOW-FREE BATH LIGHT
New to market is a new, patented, three-light bath fixture developed by Brian Hart of Forecast Lighting. Hart came upon the idea when he renovated a small powder room and realized the construction of most fixtures block light, causing heavy shadowing on faces in mirrors. To counter the problem, Hart designed Solutions, a collection of fixtures that uses the typical junction box located above the mirror in the ceiling, but offers homeowners three lights, two on floating arms that flank a mirror.

MULTIPLE SCONCES
A row of three large rectangular shaded sconces creates an elegant, dramatic, and balanced lighting scheme over a double sink. The Metropolitan Sconce from Urban Archeology, reminiscent of the upscale nightclubs of New York City in the 1940s, has a stiff fabric shade that dominates the base.

SCONCE
Bathroom lighting has come a long way from the utilitarian flickering fluorescent fixtures from decades ago. The feminine sconce is now a popular option for bathroom walls. Though this fixture looks like it could whither in a damp location, the Wilshire Sconce with its luxurious, lead-crystal, sphere design from Restoration Hardware is crafted to withstand the heat.

LIGHTED MIRROR
A round mirror, Tigris by Tech Lighting, is surrounded by a cove of diffused white light to provide both ambient light, and shadow-free task lighting. The mirror includes a transformer and nine 12-volt, 20-watt halogen bi-pin lamps. The light is dimmable using a standard incandescent dimmer.

TRIPLE HEAD SCONCE
Bathrooms are more like retreats today, and the lighting reflects that mindset. Cherry Tree Designs' Aurora 3-Light vanity light bracket (also called a fitter) holds three lamps. The design is meant to sooth the spirit and the eye with its cherry finish, frosted acrylic shades made to look like rice paper, and nickel-finished backplate.

DECORATIVE BATH FAN
Every bathroom needs an exhaust fan to get rid of excess steam and moisture, and one that has a light does double duty. Progress Lighting offers a bath fan model with a Venetian Bronze finish recommended for bath sizes up to 65 square feet (6.1 sq m) The fan takes two 60-watt bulbs.

SCONCES AND WALL FIXTURES

Adding a wall sconce or wall fixture in a hallway, stairway, or flanking a doorway or piece of wall-mounted artwork brings an immediate sense of style, balance, and glow to an otherwise empty expanse of space. Since wall fixtures lift the eye upward towards its indirect splash of light, a room appears larger than it really is. Install a sconce 72 to 78 inches (183 to 198 cm) up from the floor so you won't bump your head but it'll be low enough so it won't just illuminate the ceiling. Place a series of sconces the same distance from the floor—don't vary heights or the room will look unbalanced. Space them at least 6 feet (1.8 m) apart. If they are placed any closer to one another, the continuous splashes of light will overlap each other and the effect will look too bright.

LEFT: WALL POCKET SCONCE
A wall pocket, or quarter-round, is a basic-shaped sconce that fits into any style décor. This type of sconce is placed in an area that demands soft, glare-free uplighting on a wall. The sconce from Starfire Lighting fits multiple light source options such as a compact U-shaped twin- or quad-tube fluorescent, or a standard 60-watt incandescent bulb that all create a diffused light through the white, translucent shade.

RIGHT: ART NOUVEAU-INSPIRED SCONCE
A sconce is often a work of wall art in itself. The design of the Beaux Arts Pendant Sconce from Restoration Hardware is taken from Art Nouveau icons of the early 1900s. It has a hammered, detailed wall plate with a hand-rubbed antique finish. The diffuser is seeded glass, which makes it look like the glow of a candle emitting from the fixture.

LEFT: ANTIQUE CANDLESTICK SCONCE
The idea of a sconce goes back in time before electricity when candles were placed on holders installed on walls. This classic Colonial America-inspired version from Hubbardton Forge has a square backplate in a natural iron finish. It takes a 60-watt candelabra socket for the look of a single candle flame. A simple sconce like this looks best when used in pairs to flank a door to a dining area, or installed on both sides of a traditional piece of artwork.

RIGHT: ELONGATED WALL SCONCE
Oversized sconces can be used as a single statement or in a row down long, wide hallways. The Sweeping Taper Wall Torch from Hubbardton Forge is one such style that is large, but graceful enough so it does not take over a room or space. Always consider the projection of a wall sconce. This uplight sconce projects 6 inches (15 cm) which means it is meant for hallways exceeding the common 5-foot (1.5 meter) width.

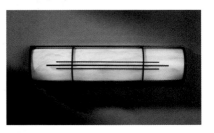

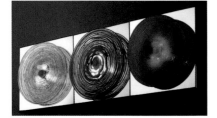

HORIZONTAL/VERTICAL SCONCE
A horizontally installed wall sconce will emit a different type of light than will a vertically installed sconce. This elongated sconce from Hubbardton Forge is designed for either horizontal or vertical applications. The horizontal version will emit a longer strip of diffused lighting that will project up on the wall and out into the room. A vertical installation will emit light to illuminate the wall on either side of the fixture and out into the room.

SCONCE WITH HALOGEN BULB
Sconces traditionally take type A incandescent bulbs, and can now take halogen bulbs. This Mackintosh uplight bowl model from Hubbardton Forge has a G9 halogen socket for a 100-watt maximum. The glass bowl in opal will emit a soft, diffused glow.

CONTEMPORARY WALL SCONCE
The word sconce is often perceived as a traditional-style fixture. This wall fixture from Leucos USA, called Brio, features a clear Venetian crystal, a vivid red, and a dramatic, black, hand-spun, glass disk floating on a stainless steel plate. The sconce emits a sophisticated glow for a modern space. This style sconce used together in a group of two or more creates a contemporary pattern on the wall.

IN FOCUS:

HOME THEATER LIGHTING

Flat-screen plasma televisions are down in price and up in popularity. Paired with the availability and accessibility of dynamic sound systems, many homeowners are turning basements (a space that is easily darkened for a theaterlike effect) and other spare rooms into dedicated spaces for home theaters.

The right home theater environment wouldn't be complete without proper lighting. Unobtrusive and dimmable fixtures, such as recessed lights placed away from the screen, give off a soft and ambient light without creating on-screen glare. A series of wall sconces add drama, a soft glow, and again, does not create on-screen glare. Stair, step, and pathway lighting illuminates the way to the restroom or the "concession stand"—a nearby mini-refrigerator or microwave oven for popcorn—to address safety issues in a darkened setting. Combined, these three elements create a true theater experience.

Serious home theatergoers will want to consider the following issues when lighting an entertainment space:

- Recessed lighting means creating holes that can detract from high sound quality by disrupting the integrity of any sound-dampening materials installed on the ceiling.
- Light fixtures should not rattle or make buzzing or rattling noises. That may preclude the use of some track fixtures or lighted fans in the space. Hanging quiet wire pendants on the perimeter of the space work well for soft lighting.
- A tiny pool of light beamed over each movie-goer's chair will make the experience comfortable if one halogen light with a glare guard is positioned over each lap area (not head area). The set of halogen lights over the seating area can be controlled by a remote.
- Controlling zones of lights in a home theater makes the experience more comfortable. Lutron's Grafic Eye product is a popular lighting-control option. Control systems require drywall removal but a radio-frequency-based system is a solution for retrofits and beefing up existing hardwired areas.

This type of home investment insures homeowners the ability to stay at home to enjoy...and hear without interruption from strangers and random ringing cell phones...their favorite flicks.

SETTING THE STAGE
Progress Lighting captures the hushed ambience of a movie house with a lighting package designed specifically for home theaters. A basic home theater package from Progress includes four recessed lights with black trim, four wall sconces, two step lights, and a zone lighting control from Lutron that allows lights to fade in and out like real theaters.

PORTABLE LIGHTING FIXTURES

TABLE LAMPS

Lighting professionals use portable lamps to create a number of interior effects. Portability offers a huge range of options. A portable lamp adds a shot of necessary color to a room, and a large fixture can act as a dividing element in a long room with multiple seating areas. If used with the proper shade, a portable lamp can be moved to direct light down onto a piece of art. And indeed, a portable lamp can become a piece of art in and of itself.

VINTAGE TABLE LAMP
Inspired by an antique French perfume bottle, these hand-blown milk-glass lamps from Restoration Hardware bring back memories of an era long ago. The old-fashioned lines of the milk-glass bases are topped with an upholstered khaki linen shade in a classic, rounded, and slightly flared shape. The illumination from the bulb reflects off the milk-glass, creating a soft vessel of light.

CRAFTED TABLE LAMP
A wood base for a table lamp brings nature indoors. Shady Lady's Natural Instincts line of table lamps combines natural elements in modern shapes with contemporary-shaped shades. The chunky design of the wood-block base has a strong enough presence to act as a space divider even though it's 29 inches (74 cm) tall.

ORIENT-INSPIRED TABLE LAMP
Table lamps can come in shapes other than the traditional base and shade. This Japanese-inspired table lamp, Aurora, by Cherry Tree Design, is crafted from cherry with walnut accents, along with paper shades. The 20-inch (51 cm) -tall fixture receives a 75-watt bulb. Its oiled, hand-rubbed finish will mellow and patina with age, creating a lamp that will always be considered a classic design.

LEFT: CONTEMPORARY TABLE LAMPS
The five table lamps by designer Ernest de la Torre each have a unique and artistic spin to otherwise classic aesthetics. The lighted easel is a piece of art for a table. The bases of the other table lamps exude luxury, such as the rosewood column lamp with insets of mother of pearl topped by a gold foil black card shade.

RIGHT: RETRO-STYLE TABLE LAMP
Recycled materials transform themselves when they are crafted into table lamps. Lampi Lampa designs table lamps with everyday plumbing and kitchen objects for a raw, yet refined effect that fits into retro and modern décor.

IN FOCUS:

LIGHTING EFFECTS FROM SHADES AND DIFFUSERS

An element as basic and small as a lampshade can make or break the look of a room. If the shade is not in proportion to the lamp or the style does not fit in with the furnishings, the eye will immediately read the room as awkward. The five classic lampshade shapes (for hard-wired, candlestick-style chandeliers and wall sconces, as well as for portable lamps) are conical, drum, rounded flare, oval and square. What's most important to the look of a fixture is the *material* and *texture* of the shade itself. The rule of thumb for bases: a decorative base needs a simple shade, and a plain base needs a colorful, more decorative shade. Another rule: a square base needs a square shade, a round or cylindrical base looks best with a round or oval shade.

PAPER

Parchment-paper shades in cream or ivory allow for a generous amount of light to diffuse through the material and into the room, creating a warm, intimate glow. This lantern lamp from Shady Lady has a tea-stained paper shade to match the rustic nature of the fixture. The illumination transmitting through the shade's material is a muted golden glow.

GLASS

Glass is a natural reflector. Glass lampshades can be multicolored, as in Tiffany lamps. This pleated glass fixture from Shady Lady creates a play of light and shadow in the room. The individual look and color of each piece is what's most important with most glass shades. If uniformity is preferred, the best choice is white art glass, alabaster, or opal glass, each of which creates a warm, intimate glow.

LIGHT SHADE

A transparent or light-colored shade lets the most amount of light through the material and into a room, and it casts a glowing halo around the fixture. Clear bulbs make a translucent shade sparkle even more. The white, flared shade on the Billy Jean table lamp from Shady Lady diffuses light upward, outward, and downward, adding luster to the silver candlestick base.

DARK SHADE

An opaque shade, whether it's a dark-colored fabric, or a metal shade of antique nickel, bronze, or antique brass, focuses light downward for task lighting or to highlight an object on a table. The table lamp from Hubbardton Forge above has a conic shade in a terra-cotta, micro-suede fabric that lets a dusky, emberlike glow through the material, and it focuses direct light onto the base to highlight the intricate forged ironwork.

FABRIC

Some of the most expensive shades are made from fabric. But since fabric is woven, light can transmit easily through the threads. White silk is the most transparent and most expensive. Linen shades have greater light diffusion than most other shades. Bleached or natural burlap, such as the shade on this Natural Inspirations table lamp from Shady Lady, is an alternative material adding texture to the fixture, and when the light is transmitted through the shade, it has a dappled effect.

BRASS MESH

Brass mesh, used as a diffuser on a chandelier designed by architect Heather Faulding, is used because of its delicacy and as a layer to both see and diffuse the crystal petals that are inside the center of each magnolia. The effect produces a dappled reflection of light onto the walls and ceilings. Faulding also uses brass mesh for lampshades, though it usually requires an extra layer to better diffuse light. A single layer of mesh shows a light source more clearly, and it looks a bit more "high tech" or contemporary. When using mesh, Faulding says it's best to use 25- to 40-watt chandelier lamps that produce the lowest temperatures, but don't let the source touch or lay too close to the material.

FLOOR LAMPS

Floor lamps make ideal accent pieces for a room, and they are excellent sources of illumination for dark corners in a space. Most floor lamps don't take up much room, but some styles are large enough to use as space dividers and though floor lamps take up little room, an oversized shade can take up precious space. If a floor lamp is close to a wall, choose a rectangular or an oval shape since it will have narrow sides and can be pushed closer to a wall.

ROOM DIVIDER
Floor lamps seem more like furniture today. The flexibility of the Dunker divider from IKEA can't be beat since it's not only a source of ambient light, but it also creates a functional illuminated wall, whether single or configured as a ganged set of lamps. The polyester fabric shade diffuses three 40-watt chandelier bulbs.

MODERN FLOOR LAMP
Though some floor lamps look like anything but lights, they add form and function into a space. The Aega floor lamp by Andromeda International (distributed in North America by Leucos USA) is actually a curvaceous diffuser crafted from hand-blown glass and sits on a metal frame with a satin nickel or satin gold finish.

FLOOR/TABLE LAMP
Not all floor lamps are tall and slim. Some are small, short, and squat, like the Jonisk light from IKEA that is a bit above 12 inches (30 cm) high. Tucked in a corner, the glowing orb with an aluminum base illuminates an otherwise darkened space close to the floor with a light that is diffused up and out of its plastic shade. It's versatile enough to double as a table lamp, as well.

CONTEMPORARY TORCHIERE
Torchieres fill dark corners with light because they put a maximum amount of indirect lighting, without glare, up onto the ceiling. The Italian-made Drink metal floor lamps from Rotaliana are shaped like 6-foot (1.8 meter) high chalices that are filled with light. The tall, slender floor lamps look as if they are formed from a single piece of metal. The deep bowl-shaped fixture takes a 250-watt halogen bulb, and is a typical shape for a torchiere shade.

LEFT: TASK FLOOR LAMP
Adjustable floor lamps are ideal for task lighting over the arm of a low chair or sofa. The Metamorphic Pharmacy model from Hubbardton Forge is designed to adjust from 40 1/2 inches (103 cm) up to 50 inches (127 cm) high. It takes a 100-watt maximum halogen bulb.

RIGHT: GLASS FLOOR LAMP
A floor lamp with an art glass diffuser becomes the focus of a room when it is placed against a solid-color wall. The Avril floor lamp by Andromeda International (distributed in North America by Leucos USA) comes with a diffuser in plum, melon, and red color combinations of glass. The lamp takes an incandescent bulb which makes the colors glow warmly.

FAR RIGHT: SCULPTURAL FLOOR LAMP
Floor lamps bring sculpture, as well as light, into an empty corner or a room. The Tall Metra from Hubbardton Forge is an uplight not used for task lighting. The 75-inch (191 cm) -high fixture includes two glass tubes in opal that each take a 60-watt bulb maximum, and includes a dimmer switch.

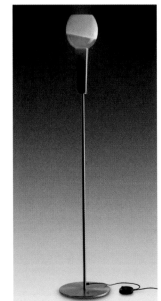

ACCENT LIGHT FIXTURES

Accent lighting is a broad category that includes architectural (hardwired, recessed lighting with a controlled beam spread or track lighting with adjustable cans) and portable fixtures meant to highlight a special feature in a room. The category shown below focuses on under- and in-cabinet lighting to illuminate dim areas, and adjustable ceiling or wall spots that can be added to a room to highlight artwork, other collections, or an architectural feature.

Under-cabinet lighting, also considered task lighting, gives a kitchen (or a home office with cabinets over a work surface) a sparkling look. They come as low-voltage puck lights (round lighted disks with halogen bulbs) or fluorescent tubes that can be plugged directly into a 120-volt receptacle. Under-cabinet lights will naturally be located close to the countertop, but remember that pucks with halogen bulbs do create a noticeable level of heat when left on for long periods of time. To better conceal an under-cabinet fixture, put it close to the front edge of the cabinet. Remember that the countertop and back-splash surface will affect the brightness of an under-cabinet light. Dark surfaces absorb the light; lighter colors reflect and diffuse light. Glossy countertops, especially dark colors, will cause glare and annoying reflections with most under-cabinet lights. For best under-cabinet accent lighting results with a dark, glossy countertop, keep the backsplash a light color.

BOOKSHELF ACCENT LIGHTING
Bookcase accent lighting is easy to achieve with portable lamps, but is almost always forgotten about in a lighting plan. The telescopic arms and adjustable shade of IKEA's Magiker fixture sits securely on a solid base.

CABINET SPOTLIGHT
Small spotlights, like IKEA's versatile Non fixture that is a mere 1 1/4" (3.2 cm) high, can be used inside cabinets, under cabinets, and inside bookshelves. Its low-level, 10-watt halogen bulbs give off just enough sparkle without emitting too much heat. The spotlight shown has a shade, but can be used without a shade for a traditional puck light look.

ADJUSTABLE SPOTLIGHT
Accent spotlights look discreet in this plastic, steel, glass, and chrome-plated wall/ceiling fixture from IKEA. It's a portable fixture, but looks architectural because of its sophisticated design. The halogen lights hang down 15 inches (38 cm), and are accessible for adjustment to highlight changing artwork.

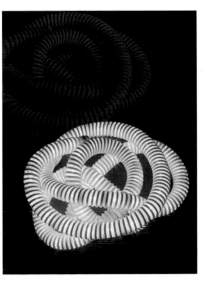

LEFT: ART ACCENT LIGHTING
Accenting wall-mounted artwork can be tricky and is always best done with unobtrusive lights like this one from IKEA. The Isfall fixture can be placed on top of a bookshelf with its shade angled downward.

RIGHT: ROPE LIGHTING
Lengths of rope lighting placed in strategic places, such as the perimeter of a cove ceiling, above windows but covered by valances, under toe-kick cabinet areas, and along lengths of tall bookcases, can create a glow that accents horizontal planes. The tubular body of Boalum, a classic fixture from Artemide, is designed with reinforced, flexible, plastic material used for diffused incandescent accent lighting. The ropes can be connected for a longer tubular composition.

EXTERIOR LUMINAIRES

ARCHITECTURAL LANDSCAPE LIGHTING

Much of a home's curb appeal depends on successful exterior lighting. Good outdoor lighting gives a home its sparkle after dark. Since the trend is to create outdoor rooms and outdoor kitchens to extend living space, planning exterior lighting is as important as planning interior illumination, and manufacturers are beginning to answer the demand. For example, the designs of exterior light fixtures are beginning to look exactly like interior fixtures, yet they are engineered with materials and designs that withstand the elements.

However, it takes a talented eye to balance the lighting needs of a landscape. When there's not enough landscape lighting, the yard becomes a dark and uneasy place at night. The lit rooms within pop into view from the road and become jarring to the eye. If the interior is overlit and there's not enough landscape lighting, we can't distinguish anything beyond our own reflection in the glass when we look outside, a phenomena known as the "black mirror effect." Too much of the wrong landscape lighting will make a property appear garish because it is flooded with bright, glaring light. In addition, too much light may cause unwanted "light trespass" onto a neighbor's yard.

The right plan combines safety fixtures (versus bright flood lights for property security) that gently lead guests through paths, up stairs, and around water features, a layer of accent lights that subtly spotlight landscape elements, and decorative entryway pole lights, lanterns, and portables that give personality to the property. It's all in the way the lighting plan uses the techniques of uplighting, downlighting (also known as "moonlighting"), spotlighting, floodlighting, and grazing. The proper mix of lighting makes the goal of comfortable outdoor living possible.

Now that outdoor spaces are becoming as comfortable and important as interior rooms, everything, including the lighting, is following suit. For example, wall surface-mounted outdoor lights now look more like interior fixtures, and they are suitable for wet locations. One of the first weather-resistant outdoor sconces, by Kichler, provides elegant incandescent light, up to 100 watts, and continues glowing even in a storm. Its body material is durable aluminum with an antique iron finish, and its shade is an alabaster swirl glass. Although it looks just like an interior sconce, the shade is solid on top so the light bulb is not exposed to weather, making it suitable for wet locations. The rule of thumb about sconce placement is the same for inside and outside installations; it should be placed on the wall 60 inches (152 cm) up from the floor.

POLE LIGHT
Placing a 2-inch (5 cm) -diameter conduit raceway under concrete driveways, walkways, or patios where you might want to add exterior lighting makes it easier to run wiring for fixtures, such as a pole light, at any point in the future. This verdigris finish pole lamp from Sternberg Lighting brings elegance to the front yard of a house. The general rule of thumb: the taller the pole height, the larger the diameter of the light circle (for example, a lamp mounted on a 15-foot (4.6 meter) -tall pole creates an 80-foot (24.4 meter) -diameter of light; a 20-foot (6.1 meter) -high pole creates a 110-foot (33.5 meter) - diameter of light).

EXTERIOR CHANDELIER
The five-tier Scroll outdoor chandelier from Shady Lady looks like it's an interior fixture fit for a dining room, but its durable black finish and weatherproof shades make it ideal for a porch or trellis. It's a bit over 27 inches (69 cm) high and a diminutive 24 inches (62 cm) in diameter. It comes in a smaller 3-lamp version.

POND LIGHT
Low-voltage water and pond lighting fixtures are installed underwater to illuminate a pool or pond, or to show off architectural or art objects underwater. An all-copper fixture, like the Cattails pond light from Outdoor Lighting Perspectives, naturally oxidizes and blends in with the surrounding landscape, and does not corrode in wet locations.

LOW-VOLTAGE PATHWAY FIXTURE
The first step in designing an outdoor lighting scheme is to ask a professional for a nighttime demonstration and insist on seeing exactly what the property will look like with lights angled in various ways. As for a pathway light, such as the low-voltage, copper fixture with a 21-inch (53 cm) -high stake from Outdoor Lighting Perspectives, it should be able to project light down onto a walkway from about knee height for safety. Ground-level fixtures, such as floodlights and spotlights, are used for uplighting, not pathway illumination.

ENTRYWAY FIXTURES
There's nothing more inviting than abundant light when approaching an entryway at night. The Aurora outdoor pendant from Cherry Tree Design hangs from a porch roof. It is crafted out of cherry and has a pearl glass shade. What makes it enticing for outdoor use is its UL Rating for damp locations. The accompanying Craftsman Sconce is also made from cherry with a pearl glass shade.

CLASSIC ENTRY WALL FIXTURE
Exterior entryway fixtures give a visitor one of the first clues as to how comfortable your house will be inside. A classic coach light, with more than adequate lighting, like this three-lamp fixture from Sternberg Lighting, gives off a warm and welcoming glow to guests entering the property.

PORTABLE EXTERIOR FIXTURES

Choosing outdoor lighting used to be simple. A few candles around the deck, a string of lights on an umbrella, or some bamboo tiki torches lighting up the pathway created an immediate party atmosphere. The trend to turning outdoor spaces into living spaces is here to stay as homeowners embrace exterior expansion possibilities, and the expectations have changed, especially when it comes to lighting.

To make an outdoor room comfortable, useful, and welcoming during late nights, there needs to be more lighting than flickering candles. As outdoor spaces continue to mimic interior rooms, portable lighting fixtures are keeping pace. Sleek, interior-style table and floor lamps and chandeliers that could sit out in the sun and in the rain didn't exist a few years ago. Now, outdoor fabrics are colorful, washable, mold-and-mildew-proof, and won't fade in the sun.

SUSPENDED OUTDOOR PENDANT
Polypropylene is the choice of shade materials for many exterior lighting fixtures. Lysta, a portable pendant from IKEA, hangs under a patio roof or down from a patio umbrella. It can be moved into screened porches, as well. It's illuminated with a 40-watt bulb for a subdued glow.

OUTDOOR TABLE LAMP
It appears as if this is a photograph of an interior space with a large expanse of windows looking out into a backyard. However, it's a photograph of the actual backyard, made to look like an indoor room, complete with weatherproof upholstered furnishings, and a sleek table lamp from Shady Lady topped by a fabric, two-tone shade made to withstand the elements.

OUTDOOR FLOOR LAMP
Floor lamps with hefty bases withstand outdoor weather. The 59-inch (150 cm) -tall Molokai floor lamp from Shady Lady stands tall in an outdoor room. The lamp is designed to look like it is crafted from bamboo.

FLOATING POOL LAMPS
What's more festive and inviting than a set of glowing, floating lamps bobbing in a pool? This waterproof, rechargeable, durable, white, molded –polyethylene, portable lamp from Metalarte/ Hinson Lighting, floats in a minimum of 12 inches (30 cm) of water and remains upright and lit for eight hours.

IN FOCUS:

WHAT'S NEW IN SOLAR LIGHTING

Solar-powered outdoor lights offer many advantages to homeowners, but the myths about them need to be squelched. They're easy to install since there's no wiring required, there's no utility bill, and the only maintenance required is replacing a battery about every three years or so. The disadvantages are becoming fewer and fewer as technology and fixture designs are upgraded. The basic plastic, black, tier, solar lighting styles are still popular, but there's a burgeoning assortment of high-quality styles and finishes available now that homeowners are putting more emphasis on landscape design.

There are still other misconceptions about solar lights: they don't give off enough light, they don't work effectively, and they require constant and continuous sunlight to work properly. The purpose of solar lighting is to complement brighter, low-voltage lighting with its softer, subtler light output to accent elements such as flowerbeds. Solar lights give enough light output to effectively mark and outline the locations of darkened areas, but they are not meant for areas that require illumination for security and safety.

To work correctly, each solar collection panel needs to be placed in direct sunlight. Then, it can adequately absorb energy from sunlight and convert it into electrical power that is stored in rechargeable batteries. When a sun-powered light receives enough sunlight, and its battery is fully charged, it can provide up to fifteen hours of accent light during the night.

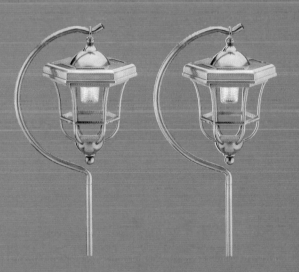

CARRIAGE STYLE

LEFT: There are unlimited designs of solar light fixtures today. Fixtures are more substantial in weight, finishes, and glass. This traditional metal carriage light from Intermatic has a pewter finish and sits on a riser or a shepherd's hook. It's used for path lighting, but can also be placed in bushes to create subtle uplighting.

TABLE LAMP

RIGHT: Solar lights also come in tabletop versions. This pagoda-style lantern fixture from Intermatic is made from weather-resistant wood. A white LED is sealed within to withstand the elements.

MISSION STYLE

LEFT: This solar light fixture looks as good as any low-voltage design. Intermatic's Mission Light has a metal frame with shimmering, opalescent, hand-cut art glass panels. Since the design of the fixture is intricate and artistic, it's meant to stand out as a path light.

LAMP AND BULB GALLERY

It's a common sight: a homeowner standing frozen and confused in the bulb aisle of a home center or an electrical supplies store. The walls of hundreds of packaged bulbs can become a blur unless you become familiar, at least in part, with the classic, and new, types of lamps on the market. There are literally hundreds of different types of bulbs available today. The bottom line rests on the bulb you choose, because that will determine the sort of illumination you'll have in a room.

For residential interiors, it all boils down to two classifications of bulbs—incandescent and fluorescent. However, there are many types and sizes of bulbs that fall under each classification, and that's why there's so much confusion. In addition, some fixtures take various types of bulbs; others don't take anything but one type of bulb.

The incandescent is any bulb with a filament inside its casing, including the common, familiar general type-A, globe, decorative, tungsten halogen, PAR halogen, and MR halogens. Halogen bulbs produce clear white light that renders color accurately, but may be too bright for rooms intended for relaxation, where tungsten incandescent bulbs would be more comfortable on the eyes. The beauty of a small halogen bulb is that it gives off more light from its tiny form.

Fluorescent lamps are not new, but there are lots of improvements to older technology and design. Complaints of noisy ballasts, flickering lamps that take too long to come on, and the original daylight fluorescent tubes that caused people to look sallow and unhealthy are now being replaced with quiet, quick lighting and complimentary warm white tones of light that nearly duplicate an incandescent bulb's glow. Bulbs include linear or U-shaped tubes, bulbs, and CFLs (compact fluorescent lamps that fit into standard incandescent sockets). The following information focuses on readily available lamps for today's home-lighting needs.

INCANDESCENT PAR HALOGEN SPOTLIGHT
The PAR bulb is a common type of halogen lamp used for display or spotlighting. A PAR bulb gives off a narrow, but not too narrow, bright white beam of light; however the lamp's aluminized reflector creates heat as well. Leucos's Flexa wall sconce takes two PAR bulbs that reflect off of its flexed steel frame.

LEFT & RIGHT: SHAPELY COMPACT FLUORESCENT LAMPS

Screw-in fluorescents can be used in place of incandescent in any standard lamp socket. Warm white tones best duplicate the glow of incandescent. Consumers who use traditional, spiral, screw-in, compact fluorescent bulbs in table lamps have another attractive option. With a warm, incandescentlike color, the Incandescent Shape lamp from GE offers the benefits of compact fluorescent technology (6,000 hours of life), but with a traditional bulb shape. This Energy Star certified lamp comes in 15-watt or 20-watt options, which is equivalent to the light output of a 60-watt or 75-watt incandescent, resulting in a $27 - $33 energy cost savings over the life of the lamp.

BOTTOM: NEW TWIST ON TRADITIONAL INCANDESCENT BULB

Common incandescent bulbs tend to produce dulling yellow rays along with its warm glow, which tends to make some colorful rooms look drab. GE's Reveal light bulb has a rare earth element, neodymium, baked into its glass that gives the bulb a distinctive blue color when it's unlit. When Reveal bulbs are lit, the neodymium filters out dulling yellow rays to make colors and patterns pop. For example, deep burgundy walls will look more vivid, and reds and blues will appear more vibrant.

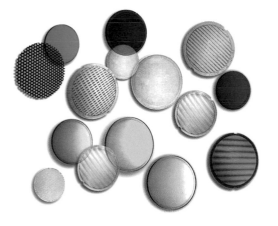

MR BULB

MR (mini-reflector, also called multifaceted reflector) bulbs are low-voltage halogen lamps that produce a spot beam of light. The bulb is mounted in a glass dichroic reflector designed to throw the light forward and heat backward. They are used instead of PAR halogens because they are smaller and the heat generated escapes out the back of the bulb and away from what is being lit. This means MR bulbs can be installed closer to what's being lit. MR bulbs produce a lot of light for the wattage since its multifaceted reflector maximizes light output. A 50-watt MR-16 produces the equivalent light level of a standard light bulb of 100 watts. They are installed with pin bases, not screw bases, and MR lamps are used outside, as well. The Mini-Underwater Lighting Line from RSL illuminates shallow ponds with a 20-watt MR-16 halogen lamp or a 10-watt MR-11 halogen lamp, and both fixtures must be used with an UL-listed pond transformer.

OPTICAL ACCESSORIES

Some halogen bulbs produce squiggly shadows caused by a lamp's filament or sprinkles in the shadows around the perimeter of a light beam caused by the thickness of a lamp's edge. Edison Price Lighting offers a selection of lenses and beam smoothers designed to diffuse a beam's hot spots and sprinkles. Color filters also clean up spots and sprinkles and add tints to make people look more radiantly healthy. Light-reduction screens reduce high-glare light output of reflector lamps by half. And, since all lamps emit UV radiation that can fade textiles and artwork, Edison Price has a borosilicate glass filter that lets more usable light pass through than plastic while maintaining a CRI of 95 percent.

"J" OR "T-4" HALOGEN BULBS

One specialty halogen bulb is also the smallest of its type. The tiny "J" halogen lamps make these fixtures from Leucos sparkle. Flut's stems of glass have small halogen lamps incorporated at the edges of the arms and Drop's luminous glow comes from small, enclosed halogen lamps. These small bulbs are used in wall sconces, pendants, and even under-cabinet housings. One issue to be aware of when purchasing MR and "J" bulbs is the pin spacing. Pins are round or square, and some manufacturers space pins differently than others. When purchasing bulbs, consider the base and pin configuration of the fixture and lamp.

MINI FLUORESCENT TUBE

Fluorescent lamps use about one-third as much electricity as incandescent bulbs, and they last up to twenty times longer. Compact types are used in smaller fixtures such as recessed downlights, wall sconces, ceiling and track fixtures. Dimming a fluorescent bulb requires a dimmer specifically designed for fluorescent applications, and the ballast must also be dimmable to work. This miniature surface-mounted linear fluorescent fixture, Tabbi from Alkco, is designed specifically for under kitchen cabinets. Its sleek design makes it barely visible and can be used where low heat is desirable. Tabbi is illuminated by a 3000K tri-phosphor 11-watt or 13-watt T2 fluorescent lamp and is UL listed for direct-wired and portable plug-in installations.

LINEAR T8 FLUORESCENT FIXTURE

Fluorescent fixtures are ideal for kitchens, baths, laundries, and workshops. But the old flickering, ghastly glow of fluorescent lamps turned off most homeowners. Today, energy-efficient fluorescent fixtures are designed to be sleek and contemporary. Progress Lighting's contoured Dome fixture is designed with a white acrylic diffuser accentuated by curved, textured, white molding. The fixture takes a standard T8 linear fluorescent bulb.

DECORATIVE CFL

Compact Fluorescent Lamps (CFLs), like this 25-watt torpedo lamp from Bulbs.com, fit directly into sockets that take incandescent bulbs. The coated CFL has a candelabra base, which means it can be screwed into any fixture, even a chandelier that takes this size base. Though this CFL illuminates a 2700K warm white color that best duplicates the color of incandescent, it may work best with a fabric shade when used over a dining table or in an entryway in order to soften the fluorescent illumination.

CLASSIC CFL

Who would think that a CFL could make such a colorful statement? Yang, by Leucos, is a table or floor fixture meant for indirect and diffused fluorescent lighting using three quad-tube, 4-pin CFL bulbs. The fixture produces remote-controlled color lights using a microprocessor and sensor for remote control activation and regulation of the light source.

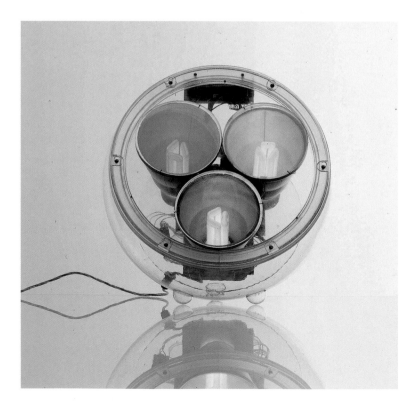

IN FOCUS:

MORE LIGHT, LESS MONEY

Walk into any lighting retailer, and you are bound to come across the blue and white Energy Star logo. Energy Star labeled light fixtures lower the cost of lighting in a home by using less electricity. Most homeowners may feel that it is already inexpensive to light their homes. Yet, according to the EPA, 7 percent of a household's monthly energy bill goes towards lighting. The Energy Star label identifies products that are designed to meet the needs of these high standards of energy efficiency. There are other cost-saving measures on the horizon. Imagine installing light under a glass floor or behind a glass wall that would last for decades, cost virtually nothing to run, and, you'd never have to change a light bulb for decades. LED (light-emitting diode) technology will make that a possibility for homeowners in time. LEDs are semiconductors that convert electricity into a single wavelength of light. They're tiny, give off little heat, and emit 50 percent more light per watt than the standard incandescent bulb. In addition, bulbs—or diodes—last 20 to 30 years, and fade to darkness rather than burn out. Because they last so long, LED fixtures can be buried in walls and floors where other bulbs could never be inserted. There's one place that takes the cost of electricity seriously. Energy conservation is critical in California, and this issue includes lighting a residence. A major initiative taking place in California could have far-reaching efforts throughout many countries that rely on electric light. California Title 24 was established to combat the serious depletion of energy, land, and water resources threatening the state's environmental quality. To decrease consumption, the California Energy Commission has initiated new Title 24 guidelines that significantly impact lighting in new residential homes and renovations. As of October 2005, builders are required to install energy-efficiency technologies in every room of the home. Depending on the room, these include: * high-efficacy fluorescents, compact fluorescent (CFL) or high-density discharge lamps, dimmers, and occupancy sensors.

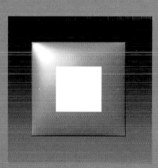

LED

The contemporary LED LightTile offers extremely low energy consumption, low heat generation, and a 60,000-hour lamp life. A highly reflective white Mylar plate allows illumination to fill the center of each tile with a uniform, low-level glow. A 6-watt electronic LED driver and quick-connector plug are provided to allow ready electrical connection. Illumination is provided by 26 white LED lamps.

REFLECTIONS ON LED

LED lights are beginning to show up in unusual places around the home. This large-scale classic Venetian mirror from Andromeda International (distributed by Leucos) takes on a modern spin with an inside rim that's backlit with state-of-the-art LED illumination. The LED reflects off the cut-glass details of the mirror's frame.

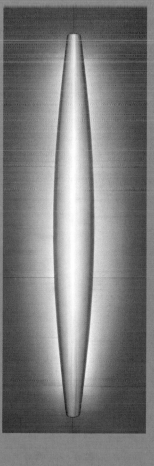

ENERGY STAR

Interior fixtures are not the only lights affected by Energy Star. Exterior fluorescent fixtures are energy-savers, but they typically cast a harsh light from under utilitarian diffusers. Ivalo Lighting's striking fluorescent Alliante exterior wall sconce is anything but basic and boring. It's about five feet (1.5 meters) in height with a powder-coat, paint-finished shade for weather resistance. The cool white light of a fluorescent lamp looks striking as it glows around the shade. It takes a T5 straight tube lamp, which will have a long life of up to 24,000 hours. This fixture is used in multiples to flank an exterior entrance, install between a series of windows, or hung on columns or on walls outside patios, entertaining areas, or cabanas. The beauty of using fluorescent bulbs outdoors is that they emit little heat and won't add more warmth to a muggy evening.

DIMMERS

Dimmers are one of the most cost-effective, consumer-friendly solutions for decreasing energy consumption. In virtually every room of the house, dimmers are the most practical way to comply with Title 24, and they are the least costly code-compliant measure. A dimmer, like the Faedra Smart Dimmer from Lutron, will save homeowners money in the long run, enhance the lighting quality in the home, and provide personalized control of light, day and night.

ANTIQUE AND VINTAGE BULBS

Most homeowners intent on creating a reproduction of a Victorian or other type of early nineteenth-century interior would not compromise hygiene and convenience in order to have an exact replica. We'd prefer a new stove instead of a coal-burning one, and a new refrigerator rather than a period-correct one to keep our dairy and meat safe. There's no doubt we'd opt for electric instead of gas light. Most restorations involve architectural moldings, decorations, and furnishings. Serious restorers, however, seek out bulbs that are as close to the original as possible, and in their search, find noteworthy alternatives when it comes to lighting a period interior.

There are enough antique and vintage bulbs on the market today to fill an entire book. In addition to seeking out hard-to-find nostalgic bulbs for sale on websites (such as eBay.com), reproductions are readily available from online retailers (including Bulbs.com), catalogues (including Rejuvenation), and traditional manufacturers (including Osram Sylvania).

To understand the market, it's helpful to know that bulb aficionados say that "antique" bulbs date pre-1930s while "vintage" bulbs date between the 1930s and 1980s. However, incandescent bulbs haven't changed dramatically since 1910. The bases have stayed the same; the Edison screw base, adopted as the standard style in the early 1900s, is still in use today. Filaments went from long, looped, and hairpin pre-1911 to the traditional coiled-wire tungsten after 1913. The only thing that tends to change now is the shape and texture of an incandescent lamp for decorative purposes.

ABOVE: ANTIQUE BARE BULBS
Antique bulbs are ideally showcased in multiples, for example in a ceiling fixture with three bulbs, like the one shown here. The bulbs are best left bare to the eye to show off their filaments. This ornate ceiling fixture from Rejuvenation comes in an antique copper finish. The three bulbs, also from Rejuvenation, are 1893 carbon filaments. Each bulb consumes 40 watts, and has an output of 8-12 watts.

RIGHT: ANTIQUE EUROPEAN-STYLE BULB
Reproduction antique rose-colored filament flame bulbs grace an Old English/Tudor-style hanging ceiling fixture from Rejuvenation. As a package, the bulbs and fixture emulate the 1920s and 1930s when Americans were in love with European décor. It was this time that Americans' newly built homes were inspired by Mediterranean villas, Tudor manors, Norman castles, and Spanish haciendas. The intended dusky mood would be diminished if modern, clear chandelier bulbs graced the rustic fixture.

LEFT: CLEAR FLICKER FLAME BULB
The flicker-flame, candelabra base bulb produces a candle-like flame effect. They differ from candle-shaped bulbs in that flicker flame bulbs have inside of them two metal plates that create a dancing orange glow that mimics candlelight. The metal plate versions are more difficult to find, but Bulbs.com's clear version has the unusual flicker produced by a photoelectric effect. Use these sorts of bulbs sparingly as too many flickering bulbs will tire the eyes.

MIDDLE: VINTAGE STAR-SHAPED BULB
Now that homeowners are restoring mid-century ranch homes, many are also recreating yesterday's mod look. What could be more retro than the once wildly popular "Sputnik" chrome chandelier with radiating arms and star-shaped bulbs from the 1950s and 1960s? The star shaped bulb, the 7-Star version from Bulbs.com, is now available for contemporary fixtures, as well. The bulb has a candelabra base and gives off a mere 7 watts, but when it's used in multiples, the effect is dazzling.

RIGHT: FROSTED FLICKER FLAME BULB
Chandelier bulbs produced during 1915 and 1916 were dipped in hydrofluoric acid to reduce glare. Today, a safer version, silicone dipped flicker flame bulbs, are available from Bulbs.com, and offer the same effect as old-fashioned lamps.

LEFT: THREAD-SPUN BULB
This Thread Spun Design, made by Spunlite and available from Bulbs.com, is a decorative chandelier bulb with an amber finish. This type of lamp, with fine spun-glass thread covering the outside of the glass and held in place with adhesive, is meant to replicate the look and feel of old-style gas flames from the early 1800s. The spun thread wraps around the bulb to create a warm glow, diffusing the light produced by the filament so it appears to shimmer. The amber color enhances the warm tone of the glow. This type of bulb is for open chandeliers.

RIGHT: VICTORIAN ERA BULB
Late nineteenth-century wall and ceiling gas lamps are easily converted to electric lamps as the hollow pipes that transported gas allow electrical wires through it without altering the look of the fixture. The bulb that replaced gas looked much like this Victorian Age Clear Replica bulb, from Bulbs.com. Throughout the 19th century, lighting levels were much lower than they are today so it is within range that this quad loop filament and brass medium screw base bulb gives off a scant 25 watts.

CARBON FILAMENT BULBS
Authentic reproduction bulbs are now easier to come by. Even the striking look of carbon-filament models introduced in the 1890s can be found to complete an old house interior restoration. This circa-1890 Edison replica from Rejuvenation has a tall, single-loop filament and can only be used in an up or down position because it will fail if used horizontally or angled. However, replica bulbs aren't known for their energy efficiency. Carbon filaments give off one-third the light at roughly ten times the price of a standard bulb and should be used sparingly. For instance, large bulbs consume 40 watts, but their output is the equivalent of a dimmer 8 to 12 watts. These types of bulb are ideally used in multiples (a ceiling fixture with three bulbs) and are bare to show off the filaments.

SECTION TWO:
PROJECTS WITH LIGHTING DESIGNS AND IDEAS

This section of the book includes projects that have been successfully illuminated with lighting plans that include a variety of fixtures, bulbs, and strategies to brighten, modernize, and highlight beautiful interiors and exteriors. The lighting, while accommodating the functional needs of the homeowners, also invites their guests in with the warm glow that comes from an ideal lighting scheme. In the following pages, architects and designers share their thoughts on what makes the lighting work, which fixtures they chose to work with (and where they found them), and how they resolved challenges of lighting the some-times inevitable awkward spaces. The projects are presented in such a way to help the reader under-stand how the architects' and designers' ideas might be adapted into other new and existing homes.

The section has been divided into six chapters according to the types of spaces we most need help light-ing: living and dining rooms, sleeping and relaxing spaces, kitchen and bath spaces, stairs and hallways, outdoor spaces, and the last chapter includes complete dwellings where projects can be seen in their entirety. The last chapter gives the reader the understanding that some homes need a consistent overall lighting scheme while others need to be taken into consideration one room at a time to achieve optimal results.

Also included where available are lighting plans and drawings that help clarify the architect's and designer's vision placement and use of fixtures and lighting techniques. The In-Focus sections through-out the chapters give in-depth information on a special lighting application used in the project. There are countless inspired ideas and practical solutions contained in the following pages. There's a lighting scheme created by a New Orleans' architect that's built around a homeowner's vast collection of black-and-white photography. Another project, designed by an Oklahoma City architect, highlights a plan where the overall lighting scheme transforms a 1920s garage and apartment into a glowing vessel that's now used as a guest sleeping quarters. The following projects from around the world show us how lighting can trick—and inspire—the eye.

Architect Rand Elliott designed this house, sitting on a hillside with its collection of lightboxes illuminating the country skies. Its ten foot (3 m) -high windows draw in the outdoors so, even at night, the distance between nature and the homeowners is visually nonexistent.

LIVING AND DINING SPACES

The good news about living spaces, and many dining spaces, is that they are mostly generous in size, or open to one another. The disconcerting news is that the larger the space, the more challenging it can be to light. Many times we choose the middle of the ceiling in a large room on which to put a fixture, in hopes that it will illuminate the entire space. We become enamored with a fixture that we must have hanging in the middle of a room, but it's often decorative and not very functional with low light output. Or, we want to update a living space with recessed lighting, but we put one in the middle of the room that beams down a pool of light onto nothing but the floor. "People rely too heavily on recessed lights in a living space," says Frank Roop, interior designer. "However, recessed lighting is not a forgiving light and should be used to wash walls rather than placed where it will downlight onto someone's face."

When there's art in a living or dining room, it presents even more challenges. "Accent lights will highlight artwork, plants, and tabletops, but if you only did accent lights, which is something I see all the time, you'd get the museum effect," says Randall Whitehead, lighting designer. "The museum effect is subtly telling family and friends that the art is more important than they are."

Of course the answer to these lighting conundrums is in layered lighting—recessed, cove, portables—that should all be on dimmers, especially in a dining area that needs mood settings. For the adventurous, there are new ways to use concealed fluorescent lighting, especially when it is color corrected or used with gels to warm up the color temperature of a living space.

Yet, how do we know when we have enough light in a large living space, such as in a loft? "This is what lighting design is all about," says Mark Kubicki, lighting designer. "There is no formula. One must assess a wide range of conditions before determining if there is enough light, and enough light for what?" There are proportions and finishes to take into consideration, too. Kubicki says that it often comes down to the "texture" of lighting. "Most offices are lit from only recessed fixtures, many supermarkets from a combination of recessed lights and coves, but you wouldn't want your living space to feel like that either," he says. And those of us who turn solely to portable lamps for a living or dining space? "Lamps and other lighting fixtures ought to be used only as tools, not as goals," Kubicki says. Read on to see how designers handled living and dining space challenges.

Although the kitchen, dining, and great
room are open to one another, architect
Laurence Verbeck used lighting inter-
twined with architectural elements to distinguish the spaces. Curved features over
eating surfaces have two layers of lighting
for the ultimate effect. Low-voltage bulbs
and hanging pendants work independently
to create mood lighting in this contemporary residence nestled in a rock out-crop-
ping in Colorado.

THE ART OF LIGHT

by Ledbetter Fullerton Architects

Keeping the lighting plan simple and basic in the contemporary home of one of the United States' most renowned art collectors was the homeowner's request. When architect Lee Ledbetter and lighting designer Davis Mackiernan began planning the lighting, they dealt with complicated issues of preserving artwork, including one of the largest and most important collection of black-and-white and color photography, in a fresh and uncomplicated way.

The interior and its art burst through the windows at night. Though architect Lee Ledbetter and lighting designer Davis Mackiernan didn't deliberately create a twilight gallery, minimal landscape lighting in the front yard and planes of light bouncing off interior walls created the effect.

CLERESTORY WINDOWS

Ledbetter was concerned that the first floor of the house wouldn't receive enough natural light if the windows were relegated to the corners of each room. To alleviate that issue, he designed a wood wall in the study that soars up approximately 13 feet (4 m) from where the ceiling of the study ends. He then inserted a 50-foot (18.3 m) -long width of south-facing clerestory windows at the top of that wood wall to bring in a flood of natural light. When the sunlight hits the sheet rock opposite the windows, it bounces light down and into the rest of the study and hallway.

WAND FIXTURES

A line of wand fixtures by Edison Price Lighting is installed on the sheet rock wall opposite the clerestory windows. At night, the stem-mounted lights evenly illuminate the first story of the wood wall as they graze the wall and matching wood bookshelves with light.

TILE FLOOR

The original floor was going to be a light Mexican travertine, but when the stone was delivered with damage, Ledbetter specified a black ash slate instead, to offset the artwork and light walls. Although dark floors absorb light, the slate does not have as much bearing on the study because the designer installed large, light-colored area rugs.

Since photography is light sensitive, that critical fact served as the basis for the architecture and the lighting plan. "Color photography is more light sensitive than black-and-white," says Ledbetter, "and we don't know what the life expectancy of color photos really is because the technology is too new and the inks are constantly changing." If basic color photographs tend to bleach out when they are closed up in albums with indirect light, how then would natural and artificial light need to be handled in this house?

Ledbetter began by designing a house with a bold-and-boxy gallerylike form that allowed him to place windows at the edge of each room. That plan accomplished two things. It created large expanses of wall space for hanging art in a way that dominates each room, but more importantly, Ledbetter adds that keeping windows at the edges of each room keeps as much harmful sunlight as possible off of the artwork.

Where glass is used, there's a two-fold protection plan in place. Each window is tinged a non-reflective bronze that works well with the green-brown color palette of the exterior brick and window frames. In addition, each window has a remote-controlled scrim for privacy and to shade art in the event of a hot sunspot.

One of the best lighting design plans is in the study on the first floor, says Ledbetter. There, he designed a soaring wall with a clerestory that runs the 50-foot (15 m) -width of the house. It's part of the architect's plan to integrate daylight with artificial light on the first floor of the house. "We designed this particular space for daytime since that's when the homeowner tends to read and work in the room." Yet there are large pieces of artwork and photography gracing its walls that have to be taken into consideration, as well.

Daylighting is the first layer of light Ledbetter focused on. The second layer of lighting in the study and in the hall leading to the study concentrates on washing walls with subtle light from wand fixtures and recessed ceiling fixtures. "Most people make the mistake of using recessed can lights that don't do anything except create pools of light on the floor," says Ledbetter. "Recessed downlights should be used correctly to illuminate walls, not to illuminate whole rooms." The whole house, including the study, uses fixtures that create subtle planes of light from floor to ceiling to highlight artwork, but without disruptive scallop patterns that are a typical byproduct of most lamps used in recessed downlights as wall washers.

Ledbetter used all incandescent lighting in the house. Ledbetter believes fluorescent lighting should not be used in a residential space because it can be too harsh on surfaces and can be unflattering on skin. In addition, fluorescents don't always adequately represent color, which was the key factor in designing this house.

All the lights are on dimmers by request of the homeowner. The homeowner didn't want to negotiate a pre-set system because he felt it was too complex. Rather than high tech, the homeowner was accustomed to using good old-fashioned dimmers to create different moods in each space.

Over the years, Ledbetter has tweaked the paint color of many rooms on other projects to get light to bounce off the walls rather than absorb into the vertical surfaces. "Bright white walls are too harsh for most homes," he says. "The color of the walls in this home is light beige with a hint of green." This subtle color achieves the same effect as bright white walls; an abundance of natural and artificial light bounces off the surfaces and into the room. "We've learned a number of things over the years about how to properly light wall surfaces by working with lighting designers and art collectors."

LIGHTING CHALLENGE

The 3-foot (0.9 m) -thick wood wall runs the entire 50-foot (15.2 m) -width of the house. This oak paneling became the perfect backdrop for the homeowner's collection of black-and-white photography. "But lighting the photography was a challenge," says Ledbetter. "Since the ceiling is designed as an asymmetrical plane, and the angle of the wall slopes to a certain degree, it became increasingly difficult to consider recessed fixtures."

WAND FIXTURES

The living room is the threshold of the back of the house that opens up into a rear garden. The room's ceiling is an asymmetrically curved vault that reaches higher up over the wood wall and lower at the exterior wall. The ceiling also leaves an intentional gap of 9 inches (23 cm) from the walls to create a floating effect. Because of its design, the ceiling became a tentlike design element of the living room, where most of the homeowner's extensive collection of black-and-white photographs is located. Rather than puncturing the tentlike plaster ceiling with recessed lighting (though it would have been easy to do), it made more sense to install surface mounted wand fixtures from Edison Price Lighting, says Ledbetter. Though the fixtures are basic models, special lenses were inserted on them in order to spread the light in a more even fashion and to minimize hot spots on the walls and on the artwork.

STRIP LIGHTING

The ceiling in the living room is held off from the walls with an intentional 9-inch (23 cm) -gap to give the surface a floating effect. The curtains were installed up above the gap where incandescent strip lighting is used to illuminate the fabric. The strip lighting also highlights the way the wall in the middle of the room doesn't touch the ceiling, but does separate the dining room from the living room without creating claustrophobic spaces.

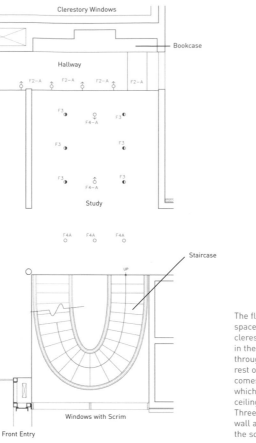

The floorplan of the study shows that the space relies mostly on daylight from a clerestory that can't be seen when sitting in the room, but is apparent when walking through the hallway to get to the den. The rest of the architectural, artificial lighting comes from eight recessed lights, two of which are accents, evenly spaced on the ceiling for little disruption to the eye. Three fixtures are angled toward the north wall and the other three are angled toward the south wall.

WALLWASHING

Davis installed three Edison Price Lighting recessed fixtures on two sides of the study's ceiling to wash a perfect plane of light down the pale beige-toned walls. The fixtures are specially designed to eliminate a scalloping effect on walls. Scalloping is distracting to the eye, interrupts the flow of light on a wall, and creates unnecessary shadows on the vertical plane the fixtures are illuminating.

TABLE LAMPS

Ledbetter rarely eliminates table lamps even from the most contemporary of any designs. "Lamps add warmth to a room," says Ledbetter. "There are so many great lamp designs today and they add a sculptural, decorative layer to a room." Here, he used high gloss white lamps with opaque shades that allow the light to be cast down onto the side tables where art objects sit.

BOOKSHELVES AND MEDIA

There was no need for lighting the bookshelves. During the day, there's light from the clerestory windows bouncing down to wash the bookshelf wall. Behind the wood door in the middle of the bookshelf lies the television.

ACCENT LIGHTING

One of Ledbetter's signature designs is to accent horizontal planes in a space with lighting. Davis installed three inconspicuous recessed lighting fixtures in the middle of the study's ceiling and aimed them bathe the large glass coffee table in a pool of light.

WORKSPACE ILLUMINATION

The homeowner uses the desk during the daytime when the task light and the natural light from the floor-to-ceiling window provides more than enough foot candles to work on a laptop computer. "I don't like overhead lights above a desk because they cast shadows of the person working, whereas task lighting illuminates only the work surface," says Ledbetter.

A CANOPY OF LIGHTED COVES

by Igloo Design Group

"We wanted to create a striking ceiling though the use of lighting coves," says Tracey Sawyer, a designer at Igloo Design in New York City. Since the ceiling of this home is visible from the street, designers Sawyer and Renee Price, of Renee Price Design, knew they wanted to create a surface that incorporated indirect lighting. "Because everything else in the home was so simple, we had the opportunity to develop a pattern on the ceiling," explains Sawyer. "We didn't want to use typical coves but we wanted to create something that was based on a standard cove detail." In addition to the ceiling's visibility and the simple elegance of the furnishings, the designers needed a well-thought-out lighting design that would also contend with the shape of the living and dining area. To address all three of the design issues, the designers crafted a fresh, eye-catching lighting plan for the ceiling.

The ceiling treatment in the living room is simple, yet unique because the designers wanted it to be contemporary in nature, but still classic to blend in with the rest of the décor and architecture. The result is a lighting design for the ceiling that captures the eye, but won't date the space.

"In hospitality design, the ceiling becomes one of the most important and easily visible elements in the design of the space and we wanted to translate that through to a residential installation," explains Price. "It is a surface that is so often overlooked in residential design and one that is usually highly detailed in other types of spaces. The ceiling of this home has high visibility from the street which meant it could not be ignored."

The ceiling's visibility was only one issue the lighting had to address. The second issue was the materials used in the interior of the home, and how to best highlight their luxurious textures and rich colors. The interior's silk draperies, hand-made rice paper wall coverings, Makore Drape wood wall panels, Italian limestone fireplace, Jerusalem Bone limestone flooring, and the mahogany and wenge wood furnishings are sumptuous to the touch. The interior's envelope and its furnishings are marked by minimal embellishment and uncomplicated lines. "We felt that the simplicity of the detailing would be best highlighted with the lighting techniques that we chose," says Sawyer. "Adding additional decorative fixtures would have detracted from the overall simplicity of the architectural elements of the space." The third issue the lighting needed to address was that of spatial organization.

The pattern of the ceiling coves was specifically designed to reflect the shape of the room, which is, in effect, two interlocking rectangles. Because of the shape of the space and its different functions, the designers needed to find a way to organize the space using an element that would not just simply relate to one area but something that would tie them to together. The lighting design provides a sense of order in the overall

COVE LIGHTING

The cove's square shape ties the dining space in with the living room area. The entire ceiling looks lit up from within, but it is achieved by the magic of dimmable cove lighting. Dimmers are important to the mood Sawyer and Price wanted to create for this dining room. The cove lighting around the perimeter of the ceiling is inherently flexible because it is on a dimmer. That way, the room glows without creating harsh glare down onto the diners at the table. Since the carpet, drapery, and furnishings are dark in color, the contrast is elegant. "We had a light-colored floor and a light-colored ceiling, medium-wood wall panels, and very light-colored finishes used in the stair area. We were then able to contrast these surfaces with darker fabrics and furniture. It is the combination of the varied tones that make the space successful," says Sawyer. "The lighting plan, therefore, had to be flexible to work with the contrasting palate."

DIMMABLE PENDANTS

The hanging fixtures, Firefarm's Small Punta de Luce pendants, provide an important decorative and colorful element in an otherwise spare space. They can be dimmed and used in conjunction with the cove lighting to suit any mood. The designers used four pendants to create a square in order to balance the room, and, because the table was square, like the dining space itself.

space while still accentuating the different seating and entertainment areas.

The floor plan of the apartment, which includes a corner off of the living room where the dining room is located, required a design that would differentiate the two areas but still work together. When designing the rectangular dining space, Sawyer and Price realized lighting would be the solution to creating a sense of importance to the area, and make the corner feel as warm and as inviting as a dining room should be. The large square ceiling cove is designed to accentuate the space and height while incorporating the lighting style from the living area.

It's intentional that there are no lighting fixtures on the walls of the dining room. "The walls are primarily windows and window treatments on the two sides, so lighting the remaining walls would have created an unbalanced feeling," explains Price. "The entire area is lit only with the ceiling and hanging lights."

The dramatic dining space is further accentuated by the abundance of drapery, but the lighting is more intimate through the use of the low hang-

ing and dimmable pendants placed over the dining table.

The city's nighttime lights don't affect the cove lighting effects. Sometimes the heavy draperies are drawn, sometimes only the sheers are drawn. When the sheers alone are drawn, the fabric simply, and softly, diffuses the outdoor light coming in. However, when all the draperies and sheers are drawn during the night, there's no worry about glare or reflections in the windows. With the exception of the pendants, all the lighting fixtures are embedded on the ceiling, and that lighting technique greatly reduces reflective glare in the windows at night.

As a finishing touch, Sawyer and Price used a tall and statuesque portable lamp near one of the windows and beside a sofa. "Portable lamps provide interest and flexibility in a space," says Price. "They can be sculptural or simply functional depending on the intent. The most important functions they have are to highlight a specific area and to create a very intimate setting for their immediate environment."

LIGHTED CEILING

The original ceiling height of the space was 12 feet high (3.7 m), but the designers dropped it to 11 feet (3.4 m) to allow for the creation of the coves and recesses. By dropping the height, the ceiling became consistent throughout the entire ground floor and gave the designers the ability to recess the drapery track systems at the windows. The pattern of lighted coves in the ceiling is meant to create a glowing background that could be punctuated with the use of portable lamps and accent lighting. The neutral wall paint and fabrics are kept subdued because the illumination is uniform and ambient, yet still creates a soft glow that bounces off the furnishings.

MANTLE SPOT

The spotlight installed far above the mantle is an adjustable multi-lamp fixture with MR-16 lamps used to highlight the stone fireplace and the art on the mantel. The placement of the fixture was important because the designer didn't want to create scallops on the wall with the light. This fixture was specifically located 12 inches (31 cm) away from the wall and the bulbs were individually adjusted to ensure that the wall and artwork below was properly lit.

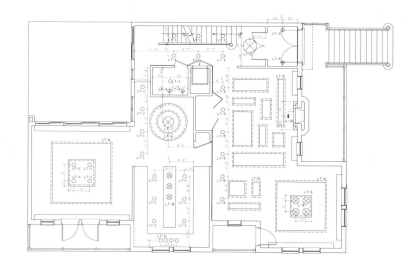

The living and dining areas are two rectangles that are connected to one another. The designers used a lighting plan to better tie the two spaces together while giving each its own identity. Though the sizes of the lighted ceiling coves differ, the shapes relate to one another. The original 12-foot (3.7 m) -high ceilings were dropped by 1 foot (0.3 m) to create a more intimate space and to accommodate the cove lighting design.

MINI-DOWNLIGHTS

The downlights used throughout the space are Lucifer DL1W low-voltage fixtures with MR-16 lamps. The designers placed the fixtures that run along the wood wall about 50 inches (127 cm) apart from one another to evenly highlight the beautiful Makore Drape wood veneer without creating a distracting scalloped effect.

STAIRCASE LIGHTING

The staircase was designed with open risers to allow the natural light from the three stories of windows beyond to filter into the space, as well as to incorporate the view to the courtyard immediately upon entry into the home. The staircase itself travels three stories to the upper levels of the townhouse. This meant that the most effective technique to light the area would be to design the lighting into the wall adjacent to the stairs. Sawyer used a simple step light recessed into the wall to highlight the steps and landings.

COUTURE LIGHTING

by Frank Roop

Pleated shades in vivid violet grace the exotic fixtures from France. The fixtures come from Roop's collection of lighting that he carefully amasses for client projects during his twice-yearly trips to Europe.

Back when interior designer Frank Roop worked in the world of retail, he instinctively knew that creating the right atmosphere in a store had a lot more to do with light than virtually anything else. He knew to put spots on certain pieces of clothing, but not to make it too bright, he reminisces. "We'd accent things to make the texture come alive, but we had to do it in such a way that made it look like we weren't trying too hard to add drama," says Roop. "If you try too hard to light something, all you end up doing is looking at the light source. A good balance of different types of lighting is the key to enhancing a room's atmosphere and features without looking like a stage set." Roop transferred those invaluable retail lighting lessons to residential interiors, such as this exotic interior in a Boston suburb.

LAMPSHADES

Most homeowners are afraid of using anything but white lampshades. One of Roop's signature designs is using lampshades in other colors besides white. He uses different colored silks in blues, reds, and bright yellows to add "blocks" of color around the room, even during the daytime when the lights are off. "The light that comes out from the top and bottom of the lampshade is white," explains Roop. "But at night, the pretty and colorful glow from each lamp creates an ethereal atmosphere."

RECESSED LIGHTS

Roop says that most homeowners rely too heavily on letting recessed lighting do all the illumination in a room, and that tends to overlight a space. Instead, Roop prefers to add recessed lighting sparingly to wash walls rather than use them for downlighting. "Recessed lighting is not a forgiving light," says Roop. Here, he added recessed lighting in combination with pieces of blue mirror. "I added blue, shaped mirrors to the top of the bookcase to add an exotic touch to the room," says Roop. "When the recessed lighting beams down on the top of the bookcase at night, the mirrors come to life because they catch glimmers of sparkling light."

CEILING FIXTURE

The star-shaped fixture is really a giant lampshade covered in stretched ice-blue silk. "It rains soft, pale, and cool gray-blue light down on the room, and the color of the light makes everyone look young," says Roop. "You'd think it would make everyone look blue, but it doesn't." The fixture hangs over the two leather-upholstered coffee tables with mother-of-pearl tiles inserted on their tops. The tabletops have a blue tint, and the soft blue light from above makes the surfaces sparkle even more. "The combination of the blue illumination from above highlighting the blue stone of the table top adds to the exotic nature of the room," he adds.

It took more than just a flair for the extraordinary to make this living room so welcoming. The giant 36-foot by 24-foot (11 × 7 m) living room had one wall of windows with a cantilevered overhang that blocked daylight, and three windowless walls that left opportunity for natural light, but gave Roop a large canvas in which to create an exotic backdrop of illuminating color.

LEFT: Roop discreetly added recessed lighting over the fireplace to properly highlight the large piece of art hanging over the mantle. "We used a basic Lightolier fixture with a small 4-inch (10 cm) -wide elliptical opening," says Roop. He then made the recessed fixtures virtually disappear by painting the metal rims the same color as the ceiling wall tiles.

BELOW LEFT: The massive 4-foot (1.2 m) -tall and 3-foot (0.9 m) -wide, custom-made lantern hangs high above the stairway. White light comes out of the clear glass top and bottom to illuminate the stairway, and a prism effect is created when light shines through the multicolored glass tiles. The 200-pound (90 kg) -fixture hangs securely by a custom-made heavy gauge steel chain.

BELOW RIGHT: Roop, as well as many designers and architects, rely on Blanch Field's expert crafting of lampshades and frames. The suede tape trim from Blanch Field was hand stitched onto the silk fabric.

To begin, Roop focused first on warming up the living room by enveloping it in neutral-toned, hand-tinted, hand-cut paper squares with a matte finish. "This technique brings a warm, cocoonlike feeling to the room to make it more intimate," says Roop. The way the light hits the wall covering adds another important layer of comfort to the space. Roop explains that when light hits a painted wall, the illumination bounces off in a very even, flat way. When light bounces off of the handmade paper squares, it becomes softer because of the variances of texture and fibers in the paper. "It looks like a stone wall rather than a painted wall," he says.

Glowing spots of color, coming from blue, red, and purple lampshades, enhances the ethereal and uncommon atmosphere Roop wanted to create. "At night, the blue lampshades create a glowing blue pool of color," he says. His lampshades are always one-of-a-kind items crafted in silk or linen, each custom designed to fit on top of a specially chosen vintage fixture. "There are about eighty vintage lamps in this house," Roop says. "I want my clients to have something different than everyone else, and one of the ways I do that is by using one-of-a-kind lamp bases and sconces that I collect during trips to Europe. In my opinion, mass-produced lighting fixtures take the uniqueness and individuality out of a home."

Roop has an affinity for the bases and sconces that were produced from the 1930s to the 1970s when the decorative arts and culture greatly influenced home décor. "I look at the lighting I collect as objects with shape and form, but I don't collect them for their period," he says. But no doubt, the form and color in every room designed by Roop is clearly brought out through his creative use of lighting a space.

ABOVE: The stairway walls are upholstered in leather tiles for their durability. Candlelight, along with the glow of the multicolored mosaic lantern hanging high above, creates an experience that gives guests great anticipation of what gems of light and color they'll find around the next corner in the house.

THE NEW FIREPLACE

by Gus Wüstemann Architects

Architect Gus Wüstemann took the top floor of an old, traditional house in Zürich, Switzerland, and transformed it with simple acts of lighting. First, the rooftop area was converted into an entirely different sort of dwelling by inserting a hammer-shaped space within the existing apartment. Then, with the magic of light and surface treatments, the orientation of the loft's old spaces changes to become many different rooms and functions as the needs arise.

In the original living area, the structure of the existing tower of the house cut into the room. The architect crafted a sculpture in Skobalit (a translucent material) and lit it up to become the new interpretation of a fireplace. "It's the overlap of old and new space and architecture that replaces the idea of a traditional fireplace as a warm, cozy element and a comfort zone," says Wüstemann.

"All the materials used in the project are raw," says Wüstemann. "Raw materials give all the surfaces more character, which in turn gives a room more atmosphere especially when it mingles with the glow of indirect lighting. Raw plaster looks more sculpted and its surface is not flat and unreflective like paint."

Wüstemann used raw MDF to craft the "hammer" shape into the loft. "It's a warm material and almost looks like paper, and the glow reflected by the fluorescent lights off of the wood is soft," he says. "The darker surfaces, such as the floor in the other spaces, are meant to create the feel of water, or a 'wave' flowing out towards the lake of Zürich; the shiny black surface should suggest a water surface and it reflects light like the water would at night."

Although the uses of each space in the loft can change and evolve, there's still the fireplace in the living space that beckons small gatherings and quiet nights spent sitting by the light of the "fire."

The structure of the house's old tower was cutting into the new living space, so Wüstemann created a negative space and then inserted a light sculpture into the cutout. The natural light that comes from the window of sloped ceiling augments the fireplace's glow.

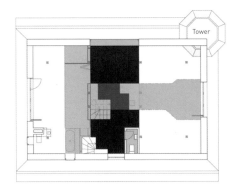

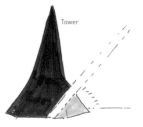

"THE NEGATIVE TOWER"
➡ LIGHT SCULPTURE

THE FIREPLACE

The construction for the lighted sculpture is simple, says Wüstemann. He used three panels of about 20-foot × 20-foot (6 × 6 m) of Skobalit, a polycarbonate material, cut by a carpenter into three triangular-shaped panels and then screwed together. Though there's hardly any heat emanating from the modern fireplace, when the sculpture is lit up with the fluorescent lights, it creates perceived warmth by creating a glowing rainbow effect.

REFLECTIVE FLOOR AND WALLS

The floor of the living space is covered in pure white Puroliss, a polyurethane material used in retail and medical spaces because it is soft on the feet and on the ears. The Puroliss material comes together with the white plastered roofline so the lines of the room dissolve. The walls, kept a raw plaster, were coated with a semi-glossy two-step varnish used for its reflective qualities.

THE SHELF LIFE OF LIGHT

by David Ling, Architect

BACKLIT SHELVES

Fluorescent lighting is used to create this lighting effect. "I start with 2,500-color temp, typically," says Ling. "If I need to adjust the color or intensity, I add gels to adjust color temperature." The alternative to backlighting shelving like this is using LED or fiber optics, but fluorescent lamps are a fraction of the cost.

CEILING SLOT

The slot in the middle of the dropped ceiling holds more indirect fluorescent lighting. The slot runs the center of the room specifically for additional illumination, and takes the place of installing a hanging or flush fixture in the center of the room.

CONCEALED TRACK LIGHTING

The library's ceiling has a number of architectural lighting features. First, it's pulled away from the walls and dropped to incorporate indirect fluorescent lighting. The dropped edges also conceal dimmable track lights that are aimed at the shelves for additional illumination.

FLOORING

The light wood flooring is intentional because of its reflectiveness, says Ling. In the library, Ling liked this particular carpet, with rich red, amber, and yellow tones, so it would bounce the light from the room up into the space and warm it up with the glow it produces.

Off-the-shelf fluorescent lighting never looked this good. But New York City architect David Ling frequently uses it to create custom lighting designs for his clients. He loves the soft indirect and translucent lighting it provides for almost any room. Whether the room is a bedroom, kitchen, or library, and the setting is urban, waterfront, or country, fluorescent fixtures have come a long way. This eye-popping, illuminated library Ling designed is evidence of just how advanced fluorescents have become. "The idea was to illuminate the library to contrast and bring out the richness of my client's collection of antique medical books," says Ling. "The result—backlit glass shelves using fluorescent lighting—provides a modern, clean, and luminous look in contrast to the vellum and patinated bindings in the shelves."

Ling says that living areas, because they are often larger than other areas of a home, are most difficult to properly light. "Most people do it incrementally, or they rely on downlights and freestanding lamps which are Band-Aid approaches and don't bring enough light from the middle of the room out to the edges of the room," he says. In addition, Ling says that most urban settings rely on hanging fixtures, free-standing lamps, and sconces because many apartment ceilings, to maximize ceiling heights, are made of rough structural slab, which make it difficult to hide conduits. In addition, urban dwellings don't have much amperage to work with, and it's cost prohibitive to increase the amount of power from the central source. But fluorescent lights work wonders in limiting situations such as these. They are inexpensive to purchase and the power it takes to run them is incidental. Luckily, Ling was able to create a

The kitchen of this apartment is primarily lit with fluorescent tubes. The upper cabinets are backlit with fluorescent lighting. Ling expanded the same dropped ceiling treatment into the kitchen where he could conceal indirect fluorescent lighting in the soffits. Since the apartment is layered with fluorescent lighting, it creates a balanced and comfortable effect for the eye, even when viewing the library from the doorway of the kitchen.

few lighting tricks using fluorescent lighting in a dropped ceiling and behind the walls of this library.

The challenges of lighting the library were in the relamping of the backlit panels as well as the spacing of the lamps so the light would appear even and balanced. The easy part was in gaining access to the back of the sandblasted shelves, he says. Ling achieved his intended effect through conducting numerous full-scale mock-ups to make sure the balance was perfect. "It became a matter of balancing the opacity of the glass versus the density of spacing of the fluorescent tubing and the distance between the fluorescent tubes and the glass. I wanted a pure, luminous surface without seeing the individual tubes, while maintaining a shallow depth-light box," he says.

PLANES OF LIGHT

by Kar-Hwa Ho and Mark Kubicki

The living room in this 2,300-square-foot (700 sq-m) -loft in a no-frills developer apartment building is designed to be a calming oasis from the outside urban noise. Architect Kar-Hwa Ho accomplishes this by giving the conventional, basic living room's shape a lighting scheme that brings an ethereal kind of warmth into the once generic space.

"The goal of this living room's design is how the use of architectural elements—such as the ceiling, walls, and floor—are used to structure the space," says Kar. He left the surfaces unadorned, but used lighting to create reveals and shadows where each of the planes interface and meet. To realize this architectural goal, Kar teamed up with lighting designer Mark Kubicki to make the planes in the space appear to float in place. As a result, the lit surfaces themselves become the sources of light in this space.

The scrims also become planes of light, even during the daytime. "The full height shades are similarly treated in all the rooms and conceptually act as a luminescent spine that threads the discrete spaces together," says Kar. "The sunshades also accentuate the architectonics of the room by expressing the planar quality of the window wall as opposed to calling attention to the individual windows."

On the floor throughout the apartment, Kar used a dark finish on the wood. It anchors together the composition by becoming a counterpoint to the lighter maple walls, sunshades, and painted walls, and it accents the continuity of the spatial flow in the apartment. It also reduces glare and hot spots by absorbing and evening out the reflected light.

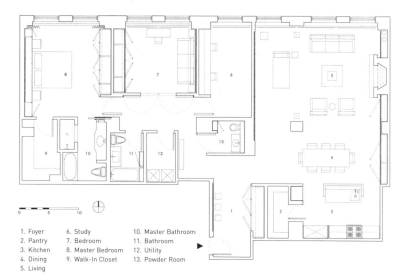

1. Foyer
2. Pantry
3. Kitchen
4. Dining
5. Living
6. Study
7. Bedroom
8. Master Bedroom
9. Walk-In Closet
10. Master Bathroom
11. Bathroom
12. Utility
13. Powder Room

ABOVE: During the day, the main goal was to suffuse the room with an even, diffused light. Kar achieved this two ways. Motorized sunshades cut down on glare, and at the same time, evened out the sunlight. In addition, the wall surrounding the fireplace is gypsum board with a painted finish so it is not intrinsically a highly reflective surface. That means that during the day, the maple panels are bathed by an even northern light that brings out the natural tones of the material. At night, the wood takes on a warmer cast due to the type of fixtures used to illuminate them.

Cove Lighting

Cove lighting is used to light the maple walls so that they have warmth and a consistent color rendition throughout. Kubicki accomplished cove lighting by using a Belfer strip light with low voltage. Halogen lamps were installed in the cove 6 inches (15 cm) on center, approximately 5 inches (13 cm) away from the wall, with a 5 degree tilt towards the wall. The rest of the walls are painted an off white and are lit by recessed fixtures specifically chosen to bring out the warm tones of the paint.

Perimeter Lighting

"How far fixtures are placed from the wall depends on how tall the ceiling is, and what is being lit," says Kubicki. "For an 8-foot-tall (2.4 m) ceiling, placing fixtures 2 feet 6 inches (0.8 m) away from the wall, and 6 inches (15 cm) on center from each other is fine. Different surface textures or lighting specific to artwork could require different measurements." Kubicki says that in this project, the perimeter lights were placed at a balance point that would comfortably illuminate future wall-hung art and also provide a bit of ambient fill light into the living area. This volume of the living space needed a significant amount of ambient light in order to feel illuminated, and the perimeter fixtures accomplished the challenge. "The fill ambient light creates a noticeably different space than the homeowners would have had if only the walls were lighted," says Kubicki. "If that happened, the space would have an art-gallery feel to it."

Task Lighting

Task lighting is used where a high level of illumination is required, such as reading. Two standing lamps are grouped around the sofa and daybed. The brightness can be readily adjusted by dimmers or switched off when not in use without disrupting the overall lighting ambience in the room. The designers used light to define discrete areas within the larger space, which gives these areas a greater sense of intimacy and variety.

Scrims

During the evening, the light levels in the loft are more contrasting than during the day. The floor-to-ceiling scrims are backlit and become glowing planes of light. They add another element of interest to the space by themselves becoming another source of illumination.

VIGNETTES OF LIGHT

by Laurence "Renzo" Verbeck, Verbeck Design Studios

"When a space is washed out with light, the depth of field is gone, and built elements are reduced—or lost—and that can be very disappointing," says Laurence "Renzo" Verbeck, principal of Verbeck Design Studios. "Overlighting is a reoccurring issue in many homes, particularly in large areas like great rooms." He says that often designers and homeowners think lighting for the entire space must be of "task level." "That means that one can read a book anywhere in a living space because it is too bright," he says. "Though seating areas need to be identified and lit appropriately, most of the environment is used for entertainment, conversation, display, and sometimes television viewing. These needs require different levels of lighting," says Verbeck, "and that can't be done with convenience store–like flood lighting," he says. "The goal is to use lighting as one tool to define space and to create moods." For this great room, part of a home that Verbeck designed in Boulder, lighting became the focal point of the space, yet it's well hidden, diffused, and creates a soft well-balanced, illuminated space.

Verbeck's challenge was to create an intimate entertaining and gathering area in a large house built in the foothills of Boulder, Colorado. The solution was to create a handful of illuminated vignettes within the large space, and gracefully do so with materials that would peacefully co-exist with the rugged beauty of the mountains and the soft pallette of the indigenous surrounding hues right outside the windows. "I like to show how a large space can be cozy by creating a compilation of vignettes," explains Verbeck. "Most people don't realize, as they glance around a well-lighted space, that the designer is directing them to the various stages."

For this space, Verbeck chose to create a design that would create interplay of space and filtered light. The unique ceiling treatment went above and beyond the typical drywall and recessed lighting. "The raised coffered ceiling, with the arching wood panels hung tightly together below the lighting creates an endless dance of edges and glowing wood," says Verbeck. The eye-catching sculptural ceiling treatment—which is essentially recessed lighting contained in a coffer—is large, but it brings down the height of the ceiling to a more intimate level. The wood panels over the recessed lights are a "rib" construction, with a thin wood sheathing; except for the ribs, the panels are hollow core, each about 2 inches thick (5 cm) and skinned in plywood. "The lead finish carpenter, A.J. of Interior Construction Services, had experience building wooden aircraft wings, and this knowledge proved invaluable on the project," says Verbeck. "I wanted the panels to have some thickness, but solid construction would introduce too much weight. A hollow assembly was the only way to achieve this design."

After all the panels were built, they were hung, each by a threaded rod, and Verbeck and his clients repeatedly tested them for spacing and

The ceiling has a large coffer built into the center of it, about 30 inches (76 cm) high. This allows the nineteen separate arching wood panels to nest into the ceiling. Each panel overlaps with others so the light can filter all around each panel. A strip of about frosted low-watt "A" lamps light the ceiling. This illuminates the area evenly with diffused soft light. The bulbs run only down the center of the ceiling, there are no recessed lights in the great room's ceiling treatment.

Backlit Onyx

Onyx is one of only a few stones that light can penetrate. Lighted from the back, it produces a warm, inviting hue with endless variation to explore up close or at a distance. Each wing, about 8 feet × 10 feet (2.4 × 3 m), has a void space behind it. The space behind the wings is an enclosed box with lights inside. The box is painted flat white for even light diffusion. Each box contains two rows of Lightolier's "click strip" of 15-watt halogen bulbs. There are two rows of dimmable, vertical click strips per side. The ceiling above each wing is a yellow-tinted plaster. The wings do not extend to the ceiling because Verbeck wanted them detached and independent of their surroundings, just as the wood ceiling panels are above. The faces of the wings are created from thick and heavy onyx panels, about 12 pounds (5.5 kg) per square foot. To support this considerable weight, a steel structure, like a window frame, was built and the onyx panels were epoxied into this frame. Each wing enclosure is accessible on the side for the light fixture maintenance.

Hanging Wood Panels

The hanging wood ceiling panels were built using a rib and thin plywood sheathing method. This is the structural core of the panels' design. After being hung and tested for spacing, structural abilities, and lighting effects, the panels were taken to a wood workshop where thin wood veneer was applied and finished. The shop owner, Kerry Stone, of WestWoods of Boulder, is a wood broker who searches North America for unique types of lumber. Sorting through his stock, Verbeck and his clients came upon two varieties of oak, a brown and white oak, along with Ceylon wood from Sri Lanka. The wood was cut into veneers of about 1/6-inch (0.4 cm) thick, which limited the lumber the architect used to just a few boards. The panels were built 2 inches (5 cm) thick for architectural effect, but they are hollow to decrease the weight of the panels. However, they are not translucent, and no light shines through these panels.

The great room is designed to elicit an emotional and dynamic response. There are six points of light in the room, including natural light, 9-foot (2.7 m) –tall vertical sconces, backlit onyx panels, a row of wand fixtures, and the dramatic light from the ceiling.

to achieve the appropriate lighting effect. Too large of a gap between the panels created glare and a line of sight to the light bulbs, which is an undesirable effect, he explains. The entire assembly was raised, and spaces between the panels were reduced, allowing for the correct indirect levels of illumination. Once the spacing of the panels was determined, they were then trucked to a specialty woodworking shop where they were finished with wood veneer.

As a sculptor and an architect, Verbeck likes to explore different materials, and his greatest joy is in bringing them to life in a design such as the unusual fireplace surround found in this great room. "I presented the concept of the fireplace and surround to the clients as an object in space, or a free-standing sculpture that would have backlit onyx wings." It became another vignette, one that would welcome guests to sit around the fireplace. And whether there was a fire in the fireplace or not, the illuminated onyx wings provide the glow of warmth for this large great room.

"There are challenges involved in guiding a client, illustrating to them early in the design process how important and dramatic lighting can be," he further explains. "When I provide sketches to clients, even very preliminary ones, I always think of how the space will be lighted, and include these ideas in the sketch and during discussions. Lighting is integral to design, period. Designers who fail to educate their clients of this are operating with a compromised pallette of design tools."

A LAYERING OF LOVELINESS

by Connie Driscoll, C & D Design

"The biggest mistake many people make in lighting a living room is in over utilizing the overhead lighting as the main light source in a room," says Connie Driscoll, principal of C&D Design. "Only using recessed or track lighting will make the room look harsh and one-dimensional." But it is precisely why Driscoll uses many layers of lighting in her living room on Nantucket.

Driscoll began her lighting plan by understanding the beautiful natural light of the island. Many of the windows of her house don't have curtains, or if they do, they are sheer to let the light inside. "The outside light plays a big role in my home. If it's a bright sunny day, no lights are needed inside. If it's dusk, the lighting is warm and low and usually with candles too—playing off the warm light through the windows," she says.

To enhance the island's light, Driscoll strategically placed both architectural and portable fixtures. There are eight recessed lights in the upper part of the coffered ceiling, two of which focus on the fireplace, two focus on the clock on the opposite side of the room, and the last four aim straight down around the chandelier. Two sconces flank the fireplace, and the chandelier hangs over the coffee table. Then, there's one tall floor lamp, five table lamps (but only two that match), and about twenty candles, including votives. "The overhead lights are always very low, and are on really to add a glow and to highlight the actual space and dimension of the room," says Driscoll. She adds small touches to bring in more shimmer to the space. In the two windows where the setting sun streams in, Driscoll has placed two glass mirrored balls, "like mini disco balls," and when the waning sunlight hits them, they make the light dance on the walls and surfaces of the living room. For measure, she placed a large glass hurricane filled with mirrored balls as a way to add more shimmer and reflective surfaces into the room. She also encases every recessed light with silver trim and baffle as opposed to the typical white or black. "This helps with light reflection, adds more of a shimmer and the light seems less direct and intentional," she explains.

The reason she uses so many auxiliary portable fixtures is because her favorite lighting technique is to use "low lighting" or lower wattage bulbs, in ancillary lights on counter tops, tables, bedside tables, dressers, bureaus, and even on the floor. Many of these fixtures are placed around or below eye level, and lampshades cut any glare from the bulbs. "All the light bulbs in my home are between 15 and 25 watts and all the recessed lights are on dimmers," says Driscoll. "People need to put every light switch on a dimmer—that's a must in my home. Even the outdoor landscape lights are on dimmers!"

CHANDELIER

Hanging a chandelier over a coffee table is a fresh place for such a fixture. "Most people would have put a fan there," says Driscoll. "But I hung it there and placed the mirror over the fireplace vertically to reflect the image of the chandelier when you walk in the room." Driscoll chose a more casual chandelier, one that isn't too fussy, but enlivened with a bit of glass beads that reflect the light. "It's just another layer of light that is not necessarily at eye or chest level," she says.

WALL COLOR

The color of the walls affects lighting—both artificial and natural—during the day and night. "Not only does the wall color change from day to night but from winter to summer," says Driscoll. "The crisp, clean bright light of the summer cools the room where the foggier and cloudier days of winter and its muted light warms the wall color." The muted color is flanked by high-gloss white used on the window trim, crown molding, and fireplace trim. "The white is so high gloss that it, too, reflects the light," says Driscoll about why she used it in strategic places. Since most of the room's furnishings are white, the walls look greener at night, she says. However, the daylight brightens the space a bit and the furniture takes on a more toned-down light gray hue.

UNDERLIGHTING A LIVING SPACE

by Simon Conder

"This is considered a radical lighting project here in conservative London," says Simon Conder of the loft apartment he designed to include concealed lighting affixed on the underside of living room sofas and tables. But it's all intentional to give his client—an artist—less visual clutter and a serene space to come home to after a day in a visually stimulating studio.

"The lighting is designed to give her a place to chill out since her daily life is already infused with so much imagery," says Conder. "For her particular lifestyle, this is what she needed." She wanted light, but nothing too obvious. She wanted the effect of a streamlined lifestyle (there are no blinds or curtains on the windows), and she wanted flexibility in lighting that did not involve portable table or floor lamps. Conder's solution was to literally hide the lights under the furniture.

OUTLETS

Conder believes in flexibility for lighting so he added a number of floor outlets about the flat. "There are about five or six floor outlets in the living room area and each is set up for data, TV, and lighting," says Conder. If the homeowners want to rearrange furniture—which is on wheels, there are plenty of opportunities to plug in and go.

LIGHTS

Fluorescent tubes are screwed to the underside of sofas and tables. The low watt lamps come in 5- to 6-foot (1.5 to 1.6 m) -lengths.

"I don't like fitting flats with decorative fixtures," says Conder. "In five years, they tend to become outdated. This sort of lighting plan gives clients more flexibility because they aren't stuck with one atmospheric style." Not only does Conder disdain trendy fixtures, but he adds that they never hang at quite the right height, either. "They always hang too high so the light bounces off of the ceiling rather than off of objects," he adds. That's why concealed lighting is Conder's preferred lighting technique. "It reflects off of flooring and furniture to add a glow of warmth to a room," he says. Although the underlights aren't dimmable, they are subdued enough to create a tranquil living and dining room.

Two glass drums (right in photo) act as huge light bulbs to illuminate the dining area at night. One drum conceals a shower and the other one is where the water closet is located. The drums, made out of sandblasted glass, are rubbed with dry white paint to get a softer color than regular etched glass. The white shimmer diffuses the ordinary halogen downlights inside the drum in a magical way at night.

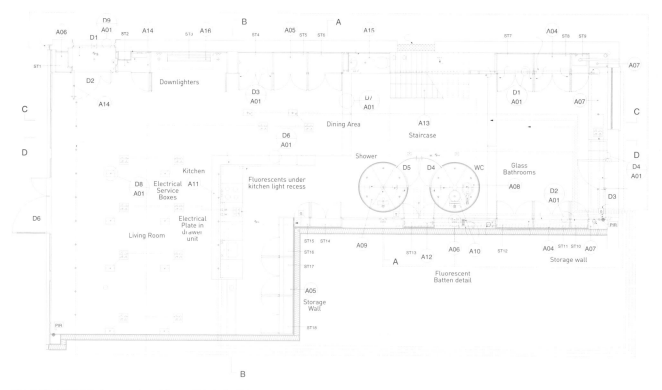

The lighting plan includes a number of floor outlets in the living room.

THE WONDER OF NATURE'S LIGHT

by Saia Barbarese Topouzanov Architects

"The living room looks sober, almost church-like, with its high ceilings and alterlike fireplace," says Saia. There is a series of eight to nine uplights that are all dimmable—above the wall of windows to bounce light onto the ceiling. The interior window on the upper right corner opens up the view to the entire length of the house and lets natural and artificial light enter the upstairs.

"Lighting should be like music for a film," says Mario Saia, principal of Saia Barbarese Topouzanov Architects. "You may not remember the music, but it's so important because it sets the climate for a movie." Saia, who dislikes "cute lighting," let nature take over when planning the lighting of this house built in the harsh landscape of Quebec, Canada.

All of the windows of this house face south in order to capture the strongest of the sun's rays. The house is seated on a stone base, and in the winter, the 1.5-meter (5 ft)-depth of this compacted stone mass serves to store the heat rays of an oblique southern sun that sweeps through the home's openings. "The 1.2 m (4 ft) -deep stone grabs energy and gives it back in the form of warmth at night." In the summer, leaves filter these rays. But the sun's role goes beyond warming up the home—it brings light into it, too.

"In the winter, the sun reflects the snow, bouncing it in through the windows and up to the ceiling," says Saia. Since all the windows face south, the intensity is bright in the living room and the kitchen where the wall of windows goes from floor to ceiling. This series of window walls extends from the living room and into the kitchen. "You feel like you are outside when you are in these spaces," says Saia. "On a sunny day, the sun makes a changing pattern hour by hour on the limestone floor as it streams in from the windows." In the morning the sun's rays play diagonal across the floor, and at noon, the rays cut straight across the rooms.

At night, the rooms, lined with fir plywood skin, become shoeboxes, and all the corners are lit to make the interior have a warm, secluded, but safe ambiance. "The most difficult room of this house to light was the living room," says Saia. "To create good ambience in a large space by using light that you can't see is difficult to do."

Doors

In fair weather, the large doors to the screened loggia open. This exterior space merges with the interior space, and the natural light filters indoors, as well.

Heaters

Discrete hanging heating lights increase the seasonal livability of the screened room.

Recessed Lights

A series of four adjustable low-voltage recessed lights augment the light from the fireplace. "You can eat and cook in the screened room, so it needed additional task lighting," says Saia.

SLEEPING SPACES

Of all the spaces in a house, it seems as if the bedroom is the easiest to light. Given all the restful styles and materials of portable lighting fixtures on the market, no wonder the bedroom is a relative snap to illuminate. But designers and architects take bedroom lighting beyond portable fixtures. It's a bit more complicated than meets the eye because although a darker room is great for sleeping, there are all sorts of other tasks that go on in a bedroom—from packing luggage to folding clothing, dressing, reading, and watching TV, which require different lighting levels.

The area above the bed is of most interest to designers today, and many are creating custom canopies of light for beds. Many are incorporating illuminated headboards with concealed lights or installing recessed fixtures over the bed itself—a technique more tolerated with the popularity of dimmers, fixtures' adjustability, and smaller apertures on lenses.

Most important, however, is a strong sense of ambience in a bedroom, created by light itself. Having too much light at the side of the beds or too much over the bed will be jarring to the eye and uncomfortable to be around. The solution, say most designers, is to use more light sources—whether it's recessed or portable—with lower wattage bulbs. That type of layered lighting will create a soothing and peaceful bedroom.

Christian LaCroix designed this petite bedroom in a seventeenth-century building in
Paris. To keep the spirit of Le Marsais, a
historic part of the city, LaCroix kept all
the woodwork and moldings intact. To give
it a fashionable twist, the designer painted
the moldings and the headboard walls a
reflective, glossy black. He installed a
recessed spot light above the window to
wash the white wall in light. Bedside
lamps, crisp white sheets, and a sparkling
original collage of the Milky Way brighten
this small room.

BOXED BRILLIANCE

by Rand Elliott, Elliott & Associates

When Rand Elliott studied the great architects in college, he'd read their quotes on the importance of light, but he didn't understand the *significance* of light. "Light *is* everything—it energizes architecture," Elliott now says about his respect and understanding of this intangible yet vital design element. Elliott's homage to the art and science of illumination is a renovated, detached 1920s Italianate-style garage and apartment-turned-guest-quarters in Oklahoma City. It's a space that Elliott and project architect Michael Hoffner designed where the floor, ceiling, and walls melt away and all that remains—during both day and night—is light.

BELOW LEFT: Since most people read in bed, it's most important to have a reading lamp. The lamp, with its long and flexible neck, adequately serves the work surface that's attached at the head of the bed and the sleeping area. Another source of soft, diffused reading light comes from the shaped light highlighting the historic photograph above the bed.

BELOW RIGHT: Elliott collected bits and pieces of interesting materials over his years as an architect. He decided to dip into his collection, found a piece of holographic film he had kept for eight years, and tested how it would react to natural light. After experimenting with it in his office, he installed it on the back of a west-facing mirror in North. The film catches the exact rays of the 4:00 PM sun to create a spectrum on the wall that lasts for just a few magical moments.

This garage apartment, affectionately called "North" after photographer North Losey, is part of a larger property owned by Losey's granddaughter. The space is essentially a 475-square-foot (143.9 sq m) -box divided into four sections—entry, dressing, bath, and sleeping—with translucent sandblasted glass panels. North is anything *but* a boring box. Though it is a simple organization of areas with clearly defined functions and purposes, it's the light which gives this place its evolving sense of space.

Elliott refers to the four separated spaces as light vessels, each created through its materials, color, and lighting. Each space, separate and as a whole, feels cool and serene, an ideal place for contemplation during the changing seasons. "The high summer sun is blinding, while the spring breeze whistling through screen wire is soothing. The fall color of the pecan tree is brilliant yellow and the horizontal winter light makes the glass vessels come alive," says Elliott. "What has been created is a place to reacquaint oneself with peace and quiet."

ON THE 2ND DAY OF THE
NEW MILLENNIUM,
OUR LIVES WERE
FILLED WITH LIGHT.

1-2-2000

LIGHT BOXES

Each area is divided by translucent sandblasted glass panels that diffuse light while offering privacy at the same time. The glass panels stop short of the ceiling for air circulation reasons, but also to create a glowing halo of light at the top of each vessel. "The vessels are soft glowing objects with a hot rim of light at the top," says Elliott. "That splash of light near the ceiling adds to the energy of the space."

FLOOR LIGHT

Wood flooring around the square column was replaced with clear glass. The aperture exposes the garage below, bringing in flashes of light when car beams reflect up into the apartment. The column then becomes a glowing architectural element that changes brightness throughout the day and night.

WALL WASHING

The main source of artificial light throughout the space is recessed line voltage halogen lamps, a few of which double as accenting wall washers. Elliott says most of us make the mistake of letting the fixture become the dominant element in a space. "Attention should be on the resultant effect," he explains. Rather than trying to illuminate a room with a single blast of light, he suggests using accent lighting, as he did when he installed the recessed fixtures around the column. These accent lights wash the column's plaster and blackboard surfaces so the architecture becomes the main focus.

There was a definitive lighting plan put in place to create this place of peace and quiet. Elliott strongly believes in having a concept in place before designing a project. "Begin asking what conditions you want to accomplish in the space with the lighting," he explains. For North, the concept was to capture Losey's legacy, and translate it into an interior space by using the mystery and magic of light.

"The interior is intended to recognize what it would have been like to be in North's camera and see his view and the way he saw light," says Elliott. "I imagine that once inside North, this must be what it is like if you are inside a view camera watching the light move past on its way to the emulsion." To accomplish that goal, the floor, walls, and ceilings are all white surfaces. "The key to the project is its whiteness," says Elliott.

Elliott designed the space so that the lights used, and the reflections they create, work in sync with the whiteness to give the space a moody, magical feeling during different times of the day and night. It's surprising to learn that there are no dimmers used in the apartment; all the lighting is zoned. "The space has an incredible amount of opportunity for changes in ambience, even without dimmers," says Elliott. The visitor can light up one vessel and keep others dark, light them all up, or keep the entire space darkened and just watch moonlight move across the reflective white surfaces.

"Rooms should have light and dark spaces for a rich experience," he adds. Without the contrast, a room will lack drama and become too monochromatic. That's not the case with North's lighting plan. "When you're in the space, thoughts of how time moves is enhanced due to the way the artificial, and the natural, light moves within the apartment," Elliott explains.

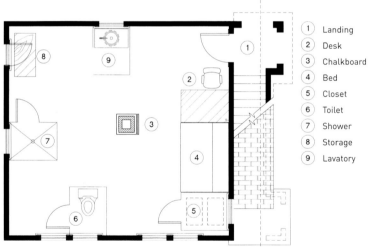

1	Landing
2	Desk
3	Chalkboard
4	Bed
5	Closet
6	Toilet
7	Shower
8	Storage
9	Lavatory

ABOVE: Daylight comes around the edges of a translucent Plexiglas panel with a mirror hung above the sink. The light frame illuminates the face with natural light. The back of the mirror, which would be otherwise boring, has a poem by Elliott inscribed on it. A recessed halogen light above the window pierces the glass sink with light; the glow of the light bounces off the white floor and softly disperses around the lavatory.

BELOW: Elliott created boxes within a box to give the square space a sense of depth. The column anchors the space. It is made of plaster, and contrasts the modern drywall surfaces. To create a light and airy sense of space, he placed the lavatory area in the part of the floor plan with the most windows, leaving the sleeping area snugly placed in a private alcove surrounded by sandblasted panels.

Reflecting Surfaces

Since all the surfaces are white, the entire space reflects natural and artificial light. "The key to making this concept work is the whiteness," says Elliott. He kept the original pine flooring and painted it a highly reflective gloss white. Both the ceilings and walls are simple drywall painted with a flat white paint.

Framing Artwork

Elliott installed a handful of low voltage–framing projectors around the space to spotlight small pieces of artwork. Elliot says the intent is to take a historic photo and create an interesting frame around it using a shaped light. "It blends a historic photograph with modern technology," he says. Framing projectors, used mostly in commercial installations, can be used in residential applications as well. Elliott specified Lightolier projectors that are installed flush to the ceiling so they blend in well in residential spaces. He recommends understanding the technical capabilities and performance of projectors because they need to be adjusted and angled a certain way from the wall in order to achieve the correct effects.

MOOD LIGHTING

by Kar-Hwa Ho and Mark Kubicki

"A room is illuminated by the reflection of light bouncing off of the objects and the surfaces contained in the space," says architect Kar-Hwa Ho. "The ambience of the room is a result of the evanescent mix of the invisible and the physical which gives the space its distinguishing characteristics." That's the philosophy Kar, and lighting designer Mark Kubicki, kept in mind when designing the lighting plan for a small bedroom in this New York City apartment.

Kar employed his favorite residential lighting technique for the bedroom—indirect lighting coves for ambient lighting along with minimal and discrete point fixtures for other illumination. That sort of lighting plan needs to be well thought out, even for a small space like this bedroom. "The most common mistake that homeowners make when lighting a room is that they leave the lighting until the last moment," says Kar. "They often think it's easy to string a couple of tracks for spotlights, or throw in a couple of switches, and they realize too late they love 'that chandelier for the powder room.'" Lighting has to be planned, he asserts: location, type of fixture, appropriateness of the fixture to the function, wiring and switching are

LEFT: The switches to the two pin spots in the ceiling are located on the underside of the two bedside drawers.

RIGHT: The headboard shelf functions as a picture ledge that has integrated uplighting with a low-voltage Xenon light strip with a series of 5.5-watt lamps placed 2 inches (5 cm) apart from one another. The surface of the ledge is made of a translucent white marble called Tassos. The light installed under the marble diffuses up through the stone and creates a warm, soft glow.

all important things to consider at the outset of designing a room. It's clear that there's much forethought that went into the lighting plan of this simply glowing bedroom.

The small glass objects and sycamore wood surfaces of the bedroom become the clear focus in the space. But it's only because of the lighting that the warm tones of the wood are accentuated to create a mellow atmosphere in the room. The designers were able to provide different lighting scenarios so that even within a small space, different moods are possible. However, the designers were also careful not to use lighting that would compete with the design features in the room.

COVE LIGHTING

Above the bed is an indirect cove light that illuminates the sycamore back panel. The low-voltage 20-watt halogen bulbs are placed 6 inches (15 cm) apart from one another, and were chosen to accentuate the warm tones of the wood. The cove-lit wood panels are a dominant leitmotif used throughout the entire apartment (see page 58–59) because they are used to define the living space and the study/guest room, as well. The lighting and material were chosen to impart a warm glow to the room and as a design motif to cohesively thread together the various spaces in the apartment.

BEDSIDE LIGHTING

Bedside lighting is served with two discrete pin spots in the ceiling above the bed. The location and angle of the light provides optimal illumination for a person reading in bed. "I prefer to use recessed fixtures without trim," says Kar. "Trimless fixtures don't interrupt the continuity of the wall or ceiling surface."

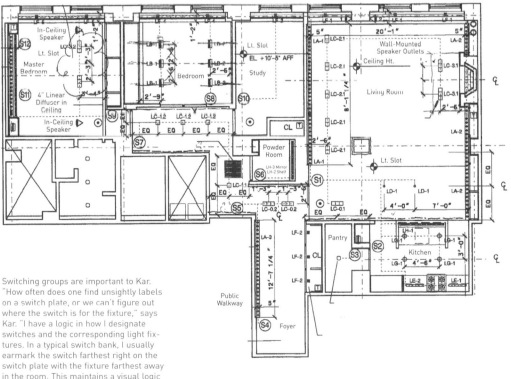

- • Low-Voltage Downlights (LA)
- ▬ Wall Washer (LB)
- ▢ Square Trimless Spots (LC-1)
- ▭ Square Trimless Spots (LC-2)
- ▭ Square Trimless Spots (LC-3)
- ◦ Semi-Recessed Low-Voltage Downlight (LD)
- ▭ Miniature Halogen Undercounter (LE)
- ■ Square Recessed Downlight (LF)
- ⊕ Semi-Recessed Downlight (LG)
- ▭ Specialty Lights (LH)
- Ⓢ Switching Groups
- ⊙ Smoke Detector
- Ⓣ Transformer
- ▯ Speaker Cable Hub
- ▽ Speaker Cable Outlet

Switching groups are important to Kar. "How often does one find unsightly labels on a switch plate, or we can't figure out where the switch is for the fixture," says Kar. "I have a logic in how I designate switches and the corresponding light fixtures. In a typical switch bank, I usually earmark the switch farthest right on the switch plate with the fixture farthest away in the room. This maintains a visual logic between the fixture location and the switches." This lighting plan includes switching groups.

A CRISP WHITE LIGHT

by David Ling Architect

MAKEUP LIGHTING
Across from the bed is a piece of furniture that combines a dresser and makeup table. To light the wall, Ling concealed a fluorescent tube to add more uniform, and general, lighting to the room.

CLERESTORY WINDOW
A bit of natural light wafts in from the sliver of a clerestory window that connects the bedroom and the bathroom. This maintains privacy while allowing the bedroom and bathroom to share daylight. "This is one way I like to increase the spatial depth of a room," says Ling.

READING LIGHT
The canopy provides reading light to the bed. For a bedroom setting, Ling starts with fluorescent tubes that have a color temperature of 2500. If he needs to adjust the color or intensity, Ling likes to add gels to fine-tune the color temperature.

"I don't like to buy lighting fixtures, I like to create light," says Manhattan architect David Ling, who designed this Palm Beach, Florida condominium. "If I specify a fixture, it has to be sculptural and if I can't find the right one, I'll design and build it." That's exactly what he did to light the condo's bedroom.

Ling says there is a lot of artificial light that was put into this room, but by using fluorescent lighting, it worked with the constraints of the budget he was given. "Although we could have designed the lighting over the bed and over the dressing table using linear incandescent fixtures, the bulb life and energy costs of incandescent can be prohibitive," says Ling. "Fluorescent lighting gave us the soft, consistent fields of illumination that were needed for a bedroom."

The main idea behind this room's lighting was to sculpt a headboard that contained integrated and unexposed lighting. It took ingenuity, but Ling was able to achieve the right color temperature of light and the perfect sculpted housing by experimenting with material and off-the-shelf fluorescent lighting tubes.

Although Ling says that there's much that can be done with the advances in technology for LED and fiber optics, the lighting can be costly to use at this juncture in time. "There are great advances in fluorescent technology, too," says Ling. "Ballast technology has improved so that they are more silent and have a greater range of control for dimming." The once-shunned fluorescent tubular bulb, previously relegated to a home's basement workshop or a commercial setting, now brings a soft, generous, and intimate light into a well-designed residential bedroom.

Ling designed a canopy that cantilevers off the headboard using ColorCore, a Formica product that has a monolithic appearance. The plastic laminate does not have a black core so the corners appear solid. If the laminate chips, only white will show. Ling used the material mostly because, done well, it replicates the look of lacquer for a fraction of the cost. The canopy is made up of two parts, each part concealing a fluorescent tube—one is an uplight, the other is a downlight. The light from the bulbs not only reflects off each other, it also reflects off of the glossy white ColorCore and spills out into the room.

LIGHT DOCK

by Ledbetter Fullerton Architects

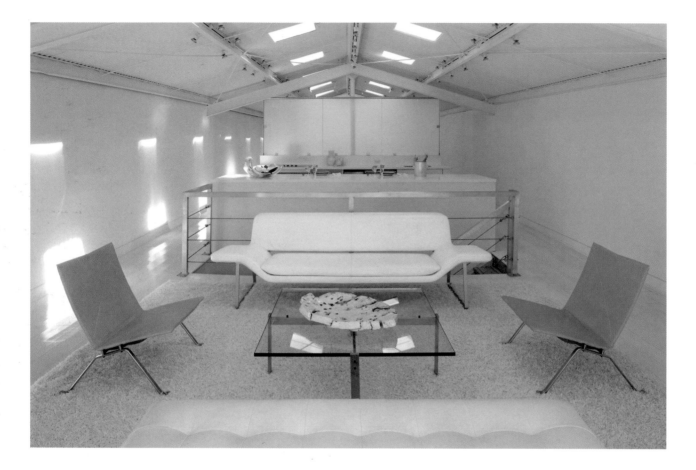

ABOVE: As the sun moves throughout the day, the light in the boathouse also changes and moves. Shadows are created and move down along the boathouse as the sun plays on each wall. Sandwiched between the stairwell and the sandblasted glass wall of the bathroom is a kitchenette area of white marble counters. The task lighting for the kitchenette comes from the track fixtures.

OPPOSITE: The exterior of the boathouse was reconceived as the most basic form of a house and executed in white stucco with aluminum channels. "At night, the box glows like a piece of ice with a green tint," says Ledbetter.

This lakefront boathouse was gutted and redesigned as a loft to take advantage of light and water views. Facing Lake Pontchartrain, in New Orleans, Louisiana, and backing up to a large marina, the boathouse is one in a row of dozens on a narrow jetty. A glass box, the bathroom floats in the center of the space and separates the public living area and kitchen from the master bedroom. The existing sheetrock ceiling was removed to expose steel beams, tension rods, and a corrugated roof. Two rows of skylights were added, and light marches through the space, emphasizing its length while enabling the white surfaces to be washed with natural light.

WALL PAINT

The white envelope is painted in "Seed Pearl" from Pratt & Lambert, but it's one color in different textures. The walls are flat paint, the corrugated ceiling is eggshell, and a satin finish covers all the structures and the wood floor bases.

THE CEILING

Not only did the original sheetrock lower the height of the space, it covered up an original corrugated ceiling and steel beams that formed the A-frame. After the sheetrock was removed, a series of skylights were punched into each side of the center ridge of the structure.

TRACK LIGHTING

Track lighting with PAR50-watt halogen bulbs (no special lenses used) is the main source of interior illumination in the boathouse. One track of fixtures was installed down the center ridge beam. On the other two beams nearer to each wall, two tracks were installed. One track has fixtures that are angled to wash the walls with even illumination. On the inside of each beam, the track's fixtures are angled to provide task lighting onto the bed, the bath, and the sitting area.

GLASS BOX

A sandblasted translucent glass box, with sides that don't quite reach the corrugated ceiling, encompasses the bathroom and separates the bed and the sitting area in this long, narrow space. The way the box is situated allows natural and artificial light to reflect off the glass, and travel over, through, and past the sides of the walls.

The goal was to make this long and narrow boathouse guest house as bright as possible. The original structure had little to be desired in the way of being light and airy as a boathouse should be. The 60-foot (18.3 m) -long and 22-foot (6.7 m) -wide space was choppy and filled with lots of little rooms, and the ceiling was sheetrocked with no skylights, which meant there was practically no natural light coming inside. "We made this into a pure white box with lighting, paint, and skylights," says Ledbetter. From the white floor to the white ceiling, and even white drapery on the window walls, each surface reflects the illumination coming from the basic track lighting system on the ceiling.

The front façade of the boathouse that looks out to a lake is now a wall of glass to let in natural light. The original pine floors were pickled to reflect incoming natural light from both the skylights and the wall of windows.

ILLUMINATING A RETREAT

by Adolfo Perez Architects

Architect Adolfo Perez always tells his clients that it's easier to install more lighting than to wish they had put more sources in after the project is finished. That's the case with this bedroom, where Perez didn't want his client to regret putting in too few light sources, especially in a space with custom ceilings that conceal most of the fixtures.

This bedroom, part of a large renovation and addition, was conceived and designed as a retreat away from the rest of the house. The former master bedroom, which was once located in the noisier front of the house, was moved to the back of the home where it was more peaceful. The homeowners, who thought of their bedroom as a retreat, especially in the evening hours, wanted to give the bed area even more of a private feeling. Keeping with that idea, the actual bed area was designed as an alcove (measuring 13 feet × 8 feet [4 × 2.4 m]) within the larger room. To give the bed area that private alcove feeling, Perez designed a contemporary interpretation of a canopy bed in curved quarter sawn pear wood that would be used to efficiently house a number of different lighting sources for various tasks and moods.

The canopy, which looks as if it is floating above the bed, helped to define the sleeping area by bringing down the scale of the alcove for a more intimate feel. It also continues the material theme of the room for a cocoon effect, while it allowed Perez to integrate a number of different lighting types into its design.

Perez created a diffuse light in the room with uplighting, which is one of his favorite lighting techniques. The area above the outermost edge of the canopy conceals cove lights, which help provide the diffused lights and appears to make the canopy float above the bed.

BELOW: The main challenge of lighting this ceiling was in making sure all the lights were mounted and located properly in the canopy. "I didn't want to make a mistake in a wood veneer panel," says Perez. "Since the canopy is curved, I was concerned that the trim of the recessed lights in the canopy would be mounted as flush as possible to the curve, which they did." Perez used Lucifer Light strips on the cove of the canopy.

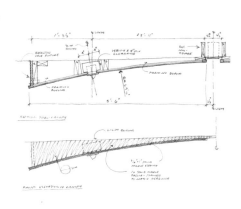

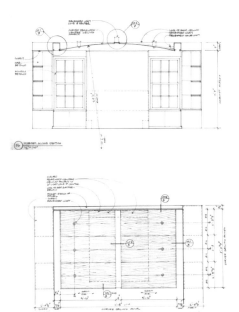

CANOPY LIGHTS

A row of mini-square low-voltage downlights by Lucifer, in black with 3-inch × 3-inch (8 × 8 cm) -trim, are used at the center of the canopy. The low-voltage lights, each with an adjustable elbow, use an MR-16 lamp of 50 watts, ideal to provide the task lighting for activities on the bed, such as packing suitcases or folding clothes.

LIGHTING THE WOODWORK

The bed alcove is lit by a number of sources, including CSI's low-voltage (50-watt MR-16 bulbs) recessed adjustable fixtures that are mounted at the ends of the canopy to illuminate the built-in cabinets. The space receives little natural light so highlighting the natural wood is all done by artificial light. The fixtures are all low-voltage halogen lamps, with warm light temperatures to closely approximate the sunlight. "Using the warmer color temperatures helps to bring out the warm tones in the wood," explains Perez.

CAPTURING DAYLIGHT

by Mark Hewitt, d-squared

WARM AND COOL LIGHT

"Both halogen and fluorescent fittings are used, and the homeowners can define how warm or cool the light quality of the space is by selecting different combinations," says Hewitt. Fluorescent units are recessed in colored boxes, which also add a subtlety to the color rendition of the space.

PREVENTING CLAUSTROPHOBIA

Light fittings in the space are set behind projections in the walls to give washes rather than to call out points of artificial light. "Setting lights back into projected parts of a room gives a sense of spaciousness in a potentially claustrophobic semi-basement by dissolving edges between binding elements such as walls and ceilings," says Hewitt.

"The project brief was complex," says Hewitt. "The client wanted to use the lower-level space as a large reception room with a capability to show movies to a high audio visual standard, but also to have an occasional bedroom for visitors, with an in-suite bathroom, basic kitchen facilities and, in addition, an office." The complexity of the space called for variations in lighting, though day lighting would be optimized.

"The biggest mistake a designer or architect can make when lighting a space is to be too monofocal about the way their clients might want to use the space," says Hewitt. "Designers often have a preconceived optimal lighting formula for a space, rather than allowing for variations and different combinations of mood and light quality."

Since the space was down below street level, Hewitt made sure he incorporated variations of lighting. That meant mixing in incandescent, fluorescent, and daylight. But it was a delicate balance based on the project's geographical location. "Because of the latitude, there is a preference for the warm colour spectrum—for example, from incandescent tungsten lamps rather than cool spectrum (for example fluorescent lamps), which tends to be preferred in Mediterranean cultures," says Hewitt.

Mark Hewitt's favorite interior lighting technique is day lighting. Was he just being an idealist when he decided to exploit the use of daylight in the lower level of a two-story Victorian townhouse in Primrose Hill, London? Not when an architect understands how to manipulate daylight by using color and reflective materials inside and out. Intelligent lighting is a subtle art, but when it's accomplished, it changes the way the space is perceived and used. That was the challenge Hewitt and his partners at d-squared had to contend.

RIGHT: Though the space is on a lower level, it's bright and airy. "This is largely achieved by manipulating daylight," says Hewitt. "Adding white pebbles to the two small yards at each end of the semi-basement, and making the floor from pale coloured screeds bounces light deep into the interior."

BELOW: One space houses a home cinema, two offices, and a bedroom. The scheme accommodates all of these demands by making walls and furniture that fold away. Color is a cru-cial device in this design: colors of all elements, such as the walls, floors, and the furniture, are multicolored, but coordi-nated to ensure that despite its various reconfigurations, the whole space remains visually coherent. Many of the light sources are dimmable so moods can shift when the walls are moved about.

BELOW RIGHT: Another way Hewitt created a bounced light effect was to apply a matte lacquer to plywood surfaces. Lacquered surfaces give the illusion of more depth. Matte lacquer, however, produces depth, but does not produce glare when light bounces off of it. The bottom of the Murphy bed is one example of matte-lacquered plywood.

KITCHENS AND BATHS

The kitchen is the most popular response from lighting designers, interior designers, and architects about which space is most difficult to light. The bathroom is the second most difficult room to light.

Because the modern kitchen is used for so many purposes—cooking, entertaining, eating cozy meals, and doing bills and homework—the role of lighting has increased in this room. In addition, the new materials being used—from stainless steel backsplashes and appliances to acid-etched glass cabinetry—impacts the way lighting is installed. Size is never the issue, say the professionals, but the type and number of lighting sources is key to having a comfortable kitchen. Many professionals today put kitchen lights on dimmers or pre-set scenes. That way, even the kitchen can become a romantic setting, or a dimmed hideaway at night after everyone else is asleep.

One of the biggest mistakes we make when lighting a kitchen is in trying to use one type of light source, usually an overhead fixture, to adequately illuminate every surface of the room. "People tend to use stadium-type lighting," says Dennis Duffy, designer, about overlighting kitchens. "Though the kitchen is a functional space, we also live and entertain there, so it's become a true residential space."

The bathroom, also a task-intensive space, poses its own problems. "It's difficult to get a balance of light around the face, there's often limited space around a mirror to fit adequate fixtures, and there are certain limits on fixtures for wet spaces," says Abby Shachat of AJS Design. "Not only that, the older we get, the more light we need in the bath." Regardless of how challenging these two rooms can be to light, the designers' work in the following pages will inspire and delight the senses.

No matter what size it is, a kitchen needs layers of lighting for the varied tasks that take place in the space. These oversized hanging globe pendants serve two purposes in this kitchen designed by Monique Gibson and Design Galleria of Atlanta. One of the fixtures gives off soft ambient lighting over the breakfast table, and the other supplements recessed task lighting over the large island. The size of the fixtures makes sense in this kitchen because of its high cathedral ceiling. The pendants' soft glow also reflects in the tiled wall with windows.

A CHEF'S DELIGHT

by Chapman Architects

Architect Meg Chapman likes to mix light sources on interior projects. A glowing incandescent source can warm up a space; an incandescent task light fulfills a function; and reflected halogen light enhances the way people and objects look. Since the kitchen she designed in this loft in New York City's SoHo section was a professional chef's domain, Chapman knew the lighting plan was of the utmost importance. The lighting would need to make the food her client prepared look just as good as the architecture. In addition, the loft is open—only the bathrooms and bedroom have walls, making the kitchen area central to the apartment's appearance.

So many kitchens that are new or renovated today rely solely on recessed downlights to do the job of what three different sources need to do to adequately light a working and entertaining space. "I think that the most common mistake homeowners make is to want and use only recessed downlights," says Chapman. "They can be very effective for lighting surfaces, but are not generally pleasant ambient lighting for spaces so I use them very selectively in my projects."

Along with recessed fixtures in her client's kitchen, Chapman used halogen and incandescent lighting to create depth in the 200-square-foot (61 sq-m) -space. Using direct, indirect, and visible light sources together enhances the materials, and the layered lighting provides excellent task illumination. "Combining direct and indirect lighting fills in the shadows that would be created by a single light source," says Chapman.

Legend

⊕	Recessed ceiling light
○	Sconce
——	Track Lighing
- - - -	Fluorescent Lighting Under Cabinet
▢	Ceiling Light
◎	Pendant Light
▫	Exhaust fan
✕	Fan w/ light

ABOVE: Halogen strip lights from WAC provide the under-counter illumination and a bit of visual texture in the kitchen. Chapman used the strip lighting to intensify the colors in foods as well as for illuminating fine tasks. The reflectivity of the materials—the stainless steel back splash and the Carrara marble countertop—were selected to balance the dark wood aesthetically rather than specifically for the lighting. However, the effect of the fixture's placement is visible. The linear fixture is installed at the front edge of the bottom of the cabinet, and the bulbs of the strip light are positioned every 6 inches (15 cm) to cause the distinctive vertical striping effect against the back splash and the horizontal graining of the cabinetry.

LEFT: The kitchen opens up into the living room of this chef's loft.

DARK SURFACES

The floor is oak with a custom dark stain, and the cabinets are quarter-sawn walnut with the grain running horizontally. Punctuating the dark surfaces are stainless steel appliances. Chapman's client preferred dusky, rich wood kitchen cabinets, but if all the surfaces had been dark, the space would have been too difficult to properly light without creating hotspots and glare on countertops.

PENDANTS OVER FLOOR SPACE

Chapman selected two incandescent pendant fixtures with halogen bulbs for the kitchen. Since the kitchen is so open, it was essential that the pendants were dimmable. The pendant fixtures light the inside of the upper cabinet when the doors are opened to help her client find ingredients. In addition, the pendants, with white glass diffusers, give off light in all directions to occupy and define the space while bouncing off the white ceiling to give the entire room a warm glow. The look of pendants used over floor space in a kitchen rather than over island space is refreshing. "I frequently use pendant fixtures to define space," says Chapman of the Milan "Rondo" fixtures from Zaneen.

HOOD LIGHTING

The halogen downlights installed on the underside of the stovetop hood fills in the task lighting that is necessary on the working peninsula. In addition, there are four downlights in the kitchen that are positioned over the countertops that have no upper cabinets and therefore, no under-cabinet lighting to help with tasks.

A RADIANT REDWOOD BATH

by Randall Whitehead Lighting Design, Inc.

The sconces in the master bathroom are actually fluorescent light sources. The warm color temperature of 2,700 degrees Kelvin gives the room an incandescent quality of light, and it also fulfills California's strict energy conservation code, Title 24 (see page 33).

A contemporary country retreat, well integrated into the surrounding rolling terrain in Northern California, was well conceived by a partnership between two independent design companies working together. Randall Whitehead, IALD, lighting designer, collaborated with the architects Erickson Zebroski Design Group to work

in simple building-and-lighting materials. The result, which is epitomized in this bathroom, is an interior that uses lighting to enhance the warm tone of the woodwork used on the ceiling and for the cabinetry.

"Having natural light in the morning for make-up and shaving is essential," says Whitehead. "The clerestory windows above the sink area provided plenty of good task light. At night the sconces take over the duty. As part of a future design phase, the owners plan on adding landscape lighting so that the texture of the greenery can be enjoyed after dark as well."

A pair of Belfer "Varial" fixtures, mounted at 9 feet (2.7 m) above the bathroom floor adds an inviting level of indirect light. A dimmer lets them be lowered to a more intimate level of illumination, helping the bath to become a cozy, saunalike retreat.

Two showerheads are placed in the middle of the bathroom, but Whitehead designed the lighting so the water would not affect it. "The ceiling starts at a height of 8 feet (2.4 m) on the sink wall and slopes up to 11 feet (3.4 m) on the high side, above the shower and toilet areas. The high wall was the perfect location for the ambient light sources, keeping them way above the water line and providing a warm glow of light reflected off the redwood ceiling," explains Whitehead.

CEILING

Natural materials such as the redwood ceilings and cast concrete walls set the rural, yet contemporary, tone of the room. The redwood floors and benches have the added benefit of integrated radiant heating. At night, the redwood ceiling and other redwood objects in the room are lit from above with a warm halogen light to enhance the color of the wood.

GLASS SCONCES

The Murano glass sconces that flank the mirror are called the "Half Robbia" by Artemide. At night, additional flattering indirect light comes from metal wedge-shaped wall sconces (not shown in photograph) mounted on the wall, called "Varial," by Belfer Lighting.

GLASS BLOCKS

Beyond the shower area is a double glass door leading to the Jacuzzi. A 5-foot (1.5 m) -high glass block wall divides the shower area from the rest of the bath. The glass block half-wall allows natural light to flow into the bath area yet still offers a bit of privacy.

A DESIGNER'S OWN LIGHTING PLAN

by Duffy Design Group

Designer Dennis Duffy had the chance to put his own lighting preferences into action when he renovated the kitchen of his condominium unit. The kitchen had little architectural interest or features, so Duffy added material detailing in the space, and enhanced it with lighting. "Lighting makes such a huge difference in an architecturally bland space, it's a tool that not many people take the time to use," says Duffy.

The kitchen, one long parallelogram, creating an angular space, proved to be the biggest challenge for Duffy. He says many kitchens are difficult to properly illuminate because the task and entertainment lighting has to be well-balanced. He says that many homeowners create an aesthetically pleasing kitchen that does not function because it's overlit. "We live and entertain in our kitchen, but we also need it to be functional for all the cooking tasks, as well," he says. "Most people don't consider the different levels of light needed in a space such as a kitchen, and instead, rely on one type of lighting source, such as one direct downlight, to do all the illumination." On the bright side, the designer says that homeowners are now experimenting with dimmer switches as they get more comfortable with the technology that's been around for over a decade, and, Lutron's Grafik Eye system is now more widely used and accepted.

For his own kitchen, Duffy needed to better balance the angularity of the parallelogram shape by staining the cabinets, floors, and walls the same white color. By creating a cohesive envelope, the kitchen still has lots of angles, but does not look broken up or jagged in any way.

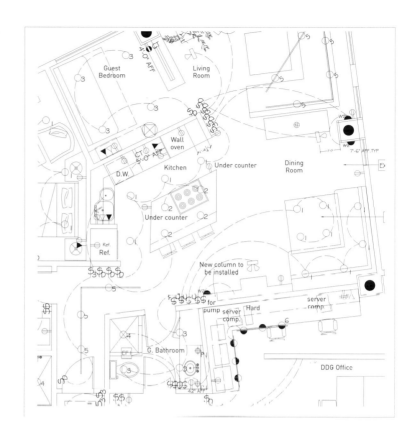

ISLAND LIGHTING

The 5-foot (1.5 m) -wide, 9-foot (2.7 m) -long island is lit for both entertaining and task work. Recessed low-voltage lighting brings crisp, clean, clear lighting down to the surface. "Recessed low-voltage lights work well in kitchen applications," says Duffy. "Though it depends on the height of the ceiling, more than likely, the low-voltage lighting will not add any heat to an already warm kitchen." He prefers to use more fixtures with smaller, 3-inch (8 cm) -wide apertures than less fixtures with larger openings. Using more smaller fixtures is less conspicuous in the ceiling than using less larger fixtures. Further, larger fixtures are not low-voltage, and that means there would have to be more line voltage added, Duffy explains. Duffy used two glass donuts (part of the trim kit) over the counter area to soften and disperse the lights. "I didn't want any hot spots on the surface," he says.

STAINLESS STEEL

When lighting a kitchen with stainless steel appliances, Duffy says the difficulty comes in how the light is directed at the surfaces. "Stainless steel has a nice luster, but every fingerprint shows up on it," he says. "The rule of thumb is to avoid glare by making sure you don't put any direct light onto the stainless surfaces."

CABINETS

The stained maple cabinets have a matte finish so light wouldn't bounce off it. The matte finish reduces glare and causes the cabinets to recede into the wall. "There's a time when you want to call out cabinets, but not in this kitchen," says Duffy. "If the cabinets stood out, too many angles would have been called into focus and the space would have looked fragmented." The acid-etched cabinet door fronts have a subtle translucency to them, but it's intentionally difficult to see anything behind the glass.

UNDER-CABINET LIGHTS

A dark granite back splash punctuates the neutral tone of the space. Duffy used halogen for under cabinet lighting. He didn't want to use fluorescent, a typical under-cabinet fixture because the light would have had a colder and harder-to-control color temperature and it wouldn't be dimmable. "Color-corrected fluorescents have come a long way, but they are still a long way from the color rendition of halogen," says Duffy.

RENEWING A KITCHEN WITH LIGHT

by Randall Whitehead Lighting Design, Inc.

When revered lighting designer, Randall Whitehead, decided to remodel his own San Francisco five-story row house, it became an experiment on how to renovate, change, and add lighting while staying sane. At first, Whitehead wanted to gut his 1980s galley-style kitchen, but that decision was vetoed because of the involved cost and disruption. Instead, he became creative by replacing lighting in the kitchen to bring the space into visual harmony with the rest of his Asian-inspired home.

Underneath the overhead cabinets is a continuous run of low-voltage Xenon lighting by Lucifer Lighting. This track can accommodate miniature clip-in fixtures that highlight the collection of photographs that line the back splash. The Aquos flat-screen television by Sharp takes the place of the old microwave oven. A new microwave oven with a built-in exhaust fan is now located above the cook top on the left. The TV avoids the reflection of the lights because the adjustable arm to which it is affixed allows the screen to be pointed at an optimal viewing angle.

FRESHENED-UP FIXTURES

The older recessed cans in the center of the kitchen ceiling were retrimmed instead of replaced by making good use of the new trims, such as these products from Juno Lighting. "These 6-inch diameter housings have been around since the 1970s and are universal enough to accommodate a wide variety of newer trims on the market," says Whitehead. "The retrimming makes older fixtures look new again." The fixtures have an updated, yet softer shoji look to them. "Homeowners now have the option to switch out the trims in their existing, older recessed fixtures for a more updated look without replacing the whole fixture," he adds. As a way to make these older fixtures more energy efficient Whitehead replaced the existing 75-watt incandescent reflector bulbs with a dimmable fluorescent variety made by Philips Lighting. The benefit is that the fixtures are dimmable using a standard incandescent dimmer and they provide 75 watts worth of light for 16 watts worth of power consumption. "Since they look just like their incandescent counterparts in both shape and warm color no visitors have ever guessed that they are fluorescent," says Whitehead.

GLASS BLOCK

Textured glass block called "Decora" by Corning Glass was installed in the wall that separates the kitchen from the entry. This allowed natural light to flow into the kitchen without letting the interior of the kitchen be the first thing to greet visitors as they arrive.

UNDER-CABINET LIGHTING

Whitehead replaced the existing tubular incandescent under-cabinet lighting fixtures that used expensive short-life incandescent T-lamps with a linear low-voltage fixture using Xenon light source. A Xenon lamp provides a warm, dimmable and energy efficient illumination that is also dramatic. These Xenon lamps last up to 20,000 hours and are fully dimmable. Companies such as Super Bright LEDS are now producing a light emitting diode version of the Xenon *Festoon* lamp which has a lamp life closer to 75,000 hours. At this point in time it is not dimmable but Whitehead predicts that a dimmable version will be on the market shortly. "A company called Tresco International introduced a fluorescent "Puck" light that will conform to California's Title 24 energy code while still providing a warm incandescent quality of light for the kitchen and a cooler "daylight" color for the laundry room," he adds.

"Many people don't know that recessed fixtures can often be installed without any replastering or repainting," says Whitehead. "We relied on a variety of decorative fixtures—uplighting and accent lighting—to create as much visual height as possible to the low height of the existing ceilings."

Whitehead decided to maintain the integrity of this 1906 building by keeping the 7 1/2-foot to 8-foot (2.3 to 2.4 m) ceilings intact. That precluded the use of pendant fixtures and cove lighting in the kitchen, and elsewhere in the house. However, the Whitehead family has a taste for Japanesque objects and coloring, and extended that into the kitchen with black noir

granite countertops, black appliances, and splashes of lacquer-red decorative accessories. "By keeping the trims consistent throughout the kitchen area, whether it was for downlighting, wall washing, or accent lighting, it helped draw attention away from the light source and towards the objects being illuminated," says Whitehead.

Whitehead proved that the look and feel of any room, even a small galley kitchen that once was stuck in the 1980s with Melamine cabinets and faux granite laminate countertops, can be transformed with new cabinet facing, a new countertop, dramatic uses of color, and especially important, cost-effective lighting techniques.

THE PAMPERED KITCHEN AND BATH

by Dwayne MacEwen, DMAC Architecture

SPOTS

A number of strategically placed, adjustable recessed MR16 spots are aimed onto the island where the food is "staged" after being prepared by the Tricocis themselves, or by caterers.

BACKLIT CABINETS

The band of ribbon cabinets above the solid cabinets is backlit. The acid-etched glass softly diffuses the lighting. Because of its gentle glow, sometimes the cabinet's lighting is used as night lights.

When venerable salon entrepreneurs, Cheryl and Mario Tricoci, decide to light a kitchen and bath, it better be done as expertly and as finely as it is in their empire of retail establishments. When the couple found 7,000 square feet (2100 sq m) of raw space in Chicago, they turned to their salon architect, Dwayne MacEwen, to bring in the best residential lighting plan possible.

Neither MacEwen nor the Tricocis were in love with the building's interior, but after years of looking for adequate space in the right location, it was time to settle on a spot and the whole team knew this apartment could be built out well. In fact, with his commercial experience, MacEwen was able to light the kitchen as if it were a 5-star restaurant. "It's a moody, intimate kitchen created through the lighting, but it is also filled with task lighting." MacEwen knew task lighting was of utmost importance for the Tricoci's kitchen. Any couple who regularly prepares dinner for 75 guests needs lots of work surfaces and task lighting. The state-of-the-art

kitchen includes anodized aluminum cabinets to reflect light, and an oversized 11-foot (3.4 m) -long granite island. But the kitchen is not over lit, and in fact, does not have any hanging pendants to disturb the clean horizontal lines of the room. "People tend to over light kitchens and they lose the magic of lighting along the way," says MacEwen.

The next challenge was to properly light a master bathroom for this couple who routinely does research and development while testing beauty care products they might choose to sell in their salons. The bath, open to the master suite and the master closet, follows the form of the kitchen, and disallows for any fancy fixtures—except for a pair of dimmable walls sconces—or complicated lighting. There are recessed MR16 lights in the ceiling in strategic areas that won't create glare or hot spots on the large vanity mirror, or on the white Carrara marble floor or the oversized marble tub set under the window.

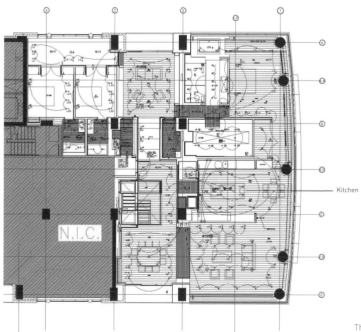

Kitchen

The plan for Tricoci's well-illuminated kitchen.

The bathroom has about four to five light switches in it for heavy control of illumination in this room. "One of the cabinets opens up and there's a single light inside of it," says MacEwen. "This way anyone using the bath wouldn't have to turn on all the lights to disturb anyone in the bedroom."

A WELL-LIT CLOSET

"Walking into a closet should be like walking into a store," says architect Dwayne MacEwen. "A closet is more than just a vessel to store clothing in."

A closet, whether it's a large walk-in, small walk-in, or basic shallow space, needs adequate, layered lighting. "You need ambient lighting and spots around the perimeter so there are no sharp shadows," says MacEwen. "If there are shadows in a closet, you may end up picking out a black suit then go outside and realize that you're actually wearing a blue suit!"

Creating a retail-like environment is exactly what MacEwen did for his client's master closet, a tall 7-foot (2.1 m) -high space that had mechanical equipment housed in its ceiling. Since the ceiling served as an access to the service equipment, MacEwen had to find a way to illuminate the ceiling. He backlit the ceiling by making a linen resin diffuser panel to place over color-corrected fluorescent strips (that let the homeowners see the true colors of their clothing better) and then placed a latticework of American cherry wood over the panel for a finished look. "We could have lowered the ceiling and put in wall sconces and recessed lighting, but we wanted to take advantage of the closet's height." A once dark, dim room became a light, bright master closet.

But MacEwen has more hints on how to better illuminate a closet. Since there are more tasks that go on in a closet than merely choosing clothes and shoes—such as looking for lint, looking in the mirror, and steaming clothes, the proper lighting is necessary to fill in shadows. Therefore walk-in closets should be outfitted with adjustable, recessed, but low-voltage lights (less heat that is near clothing) that offer cross and down-lighting on the clothing, the benches, and on the full-length mirror. Never aim the light directly on the mirror because glare will ruin any chance you have of choosing a correct color suit.

In addition to the backlit trellis ceiling of this walk-in closet, three gangs of recessed lights are placed directly in front of the clothing in order to have brighter light to distinguish colors. The recessed lights are angled onto the clothing for better color rendition.

STAIRS AND HALLS

Stairs and halls seem so easy to light; we think one fixture should take care of all the space's lighting needs. What happens is that we underlight these spaces. "Stairs and halls are often ill-lit," says designer Ed Grogan of Designworker. "Sometimes it's hard to fit in recessed lights, or small tracks are necessary. But you can still have fun in even relatively small spaces such as these."

It can be fun, if you think outside the stairway. Why just hang a light when you can use low voltage fixtures to illuminate the steps or the banister itself? Why use a straight track down a hallway when a curved one will give you not only more architectural interest, but also more fixtures for a dazzling presentation?

There are short hallways as well as long hallways that need different lighting treatments, especially if there is artwork or collections that need to be highlighted with special lighting. Why not illuminate the lines of a hallway's ceiling by concealing reflective tubular uplights? Of course halls and stairwells are not always on an outside wall of a home, which means that there is little if no natural light coming in from windows. When these spaces are located in the middle of a home's volume, then adequate lighting is of more importance.

Then there are the everyday functional aspects of lighting stairs and halls. Always light stairways from top to bottom and hallways from end to end by installing wall or ceiling fixtures every 8 to 10 feet (2.4 to 3 m). Remember to install switches on each end of the stair and hall for easy access. And the best tip of all—paint the envelope and carpet stairs in light colors for safety reasons and to help light reflect off the surfaces.

A large custom-designed lighting fixture that houses numerous hanging glass pendants gives this two-story space its dynamic character. "In a space this tall, we expect to use one fixture, but we wanted to animate the space with color and numerous lights," says Tom Catalano, architect of this home in Weston, Massachusetts. The fixture illuminates the hallway and library that wraps around the open space on the second floor, and hangs above the breakfast room.

A FLOATING STAIRWAY

by Laurence "Renzo" Verbeck, Verbeck Design Studios

STARRY CEILING

The atrium's magical environment is enhanced with "twinkle lights" that were created by installing hundreds of LEDs on painted foam panels that were mounted in an aluminum framework that was hung from the ceiling. "The LEDs are controlled by the Vantage lighting computer system," says Verbeck. "It's set to cycle randomly so the ceiling looks like a field of stars."

LED GLOWING EFFECTS

At night, the lit up-stair treads glow a soft blue-white tint. When the stairway is lit up during the evening hours, the steel stair structure virtually disappears from view. Because the stair structure recedes into the background, the glow sets off the intricate metal work of the banister.

"I believe that transitional spaces, such as foyers, mud rooms, or circulation areas like hallways, are almost always underlit," says Laurence "Renzo" Verbeck, principal of Verbeck Design in Boulder, Colorado. It's clear that Verbeck took the large transitional space of this house he designed and created a magical environment through the innovative use of LED lighting.

The 900-square-foot (275 sq m), fully landscaped atrium, with its gentle two-story waterfall tumbling through to a pond, is open and visually accessible from every direction in the house. "From the great room or master bedroom, all of the plantings, the waterfall and the pond are clearly accessible," says Verbeck. He needed to design a stairway, but he didn't want to clutter the space with a visually heavy stair structure. His thinking led to the concept of a seemingly floating stairway that would look as though it wasn't disturbing the natural environment. The result was a metal-framed staircase with lighted treads. "I felt that illuminating the acrylic treads was the best and most dramatic way to achieve this effect," he explains.

The atrium of this house does not have a typical staircase. However, the lighting treatment of the stair treads takes LED lighting to its next, and most obtainable level in residential interior use. "My first choice for lighting the treads was to use fiber optic lighting," says Verbeck. "After some exploration and experimentation, the clients—who are both engineers—built strips, each with 36 LED bulbs per tread, which we ultimately mounted on the back of each stair."

The beauty of LED lights, says Verbeck, is that they are relatively inexpensive, they are easy to customize both in the size of the groupings of bulbs (more LED bulbs equals more light) and color of bulbs, and the lights last for 100,000 hours. He adds, "The longevity of LED lamp life is an important feature in hard-to-reach areas, such as stair treads that are nestled in greenery."

The effect of LED lighting at night is brilliant, Verbeck says. Multiple settings were programmed into a computerized lighting system. "The night setting I prefer has the twinkle lights moving in a slow pattern and the tread lights lit by the LEDs with the remaining lights very low," Verbeck says. "When the other lights in the atrium and the surrounding rooms are low, the treads glow a soft, pastel, bluelike cloud you'd imagine in a dream."

THE LIGHT DOWN THE HALL

by Janet Lennox Moyer

Although Janet Lennox Moyer, lighting designer, almost never uses fiber optic lighting, she needed to use it in the hallway of this Connecticut home. "Fiber optic lighting has a real advantage when it comes to lighting tight spaces," she says. "The fiber optic fixtures are small, and they don't produce any heat in the cabinets, so it made sense for the cabinetry in this hallway."

Fiber optic lighting is best used for special spot lighting, such as for jewelry, food, and any other place that needs a remote lighting source. It's expensive and not as efficient as up-and-coming LED lighting; however, Moyer says the fiber optic source was ideal to illuminate the silver objects in the cabinets. The cabinets, with three sides of glass, were only about 6 inches (15 cm) -deep, making it difficult to place halogen or fluorescent fixtures, which are significantly larger, in the available space. The miniature track allowed a series of end-lit fiber heads that had adjustability to aim onto objects set in various locations on the shelves.

BELOW: The Lightly Expressed bronze track and heads come from Fiberstars. The elegant track can handle multiple heads (the quantity is determined by the size of the fibers and the distance from the remotely located illuminator), which are also flexible for placing direct aim on objects. The light shines through fiber optic cable illuminating the objects in the cabinet with a cool, crisp light that complements the silver pieces.

ILLUMINATING THE CEILING

The architectural details of the ceiling are highlighted with simple incandescent strip lighting placed on top of the crown molding of the cabinetry. The lights reflect up and off the ceiling to show the angled shapes.

A VISUAL DESTINATION

Using light, Moyer created a visual destination at the end of the hallway where there is a niche with a sculpture of an Indian deity. Through this layered lighting effect, the hallway has balanced lighting, and just the right amount of contrast, yet the eye is still guided to the end of the hall and the piece of art.

NIGHT LIGHT

by Ed Hogan, Designworker

Designer Ed Hogan prefers to create custom lighting designs for his residential and retail clients. So when one of his clients asked him for a banister that was lit from underneath by an old-fashioned tubular fixture, Hogan knew a new and improved version could be fabricated once he talked with one of his cherished machinists with whom he'd developed relationships with over the years.

"When you work with good machinists, you can usually get anything you want," says Hogan about how he arrived at this illuminated stair banister. He worked with machinist Philip Mocafsky, who regrettably retired, to make this bare aluminum structure that includes a bracket that holds the tunnel in which the wiring runs. "There are no visible wires anywhere," says Hogan. "The fixture is hard-wired to the wall and wires are all concealed."

The result is a clean line of light that runs down this particular part of the stairwell. The stairwell is augmented by a small MR-16 Monopoint fixture. The clients wanted to use this banister as a night light, as well. "Sometimes this is the only light they'll have on at night," says Hogan.

ALUMINUM

Hogan's clients requested aluminum that was not anodized because they preferred a bare, rough look to the banister that matched their art collection and more contemporary tastes. "The look of this aluminum with light has a wonderful clean quality to it," says Hogan.

BULBS

The fixture, which is embedded with three rows of incandescent lights, produces halos on the walls that bounce off of the raw aluminum material. But all that the eye sees is the glow itself.

WIRES

The wall is hardwired for this wall fixture/banister. The four brackets that hold the banister to the wall are also the places—or outlets—where the wires are run from. To turn on the banister, there are switches at the top and bottom of the stairs.

WALLS OF LIGHT

by Dwayne MacEwen, DMAC Architecture

CEILING LIGHTS

The staircase was lit by means of a recessed light cove at the back wall of the opening. Dimmable lights provide a path of lighting without over-illuminating and disrupting the carefully choreographed mood lighting. "When mood lighting is established in a space, it is disruptive to have to be forced to walk through or over another space that is too bright," says MacEwen.

DRAPERY

MacEwen borrowed a technique from theater production artists by using drapery as a sort of backlit scrim cloth to bring natural light into the stairwell during the day, and artificial light into the space at night. "At night, when there's more illumination outside, it backlights the drapery," says MacEwen. When the drapes are open, the skyline is still clear from indoors because the lighting in the stairwell is lower in level than the artificial city lights. Whether it is day or night, there's always a white light effect at the windows that flow down all three parts of the stairwell.

BANISTER

The handrail wall of the white Carrara marble staircase is glass. "We thought we would have to helicopter in the glass," says MacEwen. "It had to stay in one piece and would not fit on the elevator. But, we managed to get it into the space by hanging it from the bottom of the elevator." He chose glass as another way to remove vertical obstructions and to keep the views and flow of light unencumbered. "I wanted to make sure we kept the darkened part of the lower level light and airy, and one way was to bring down light from above," he says.

TREADS

MacEwen specified white Carrara marble, not only for its high-end, luxury look, but its light-reflecting appeal, as well. The white light that backlights the drapery softly bounces off the treads to create an extra, yet subtle, glow in the stairwell.

Dwayne MacEwen's clients had certainly found a penthouse apartment with adequate space, but the proposed build out plan a duplex with a less than inspiring and ill-lit staircase. Upon seeing the raw space the architect realized the best way to organize the 7,000 square-foot (2,134 sq m) -space was to use the stairwell and design it so that it was light, bright, and above all, elegant.

The stairway became the core of the penthouse. As the organizing component of the space, it houses a laundry room and closets, then leads up to a mezzanine level sheathed in cherry wood storage closet space. Building off of that mezzanine is the last set of steps leading up to the living area, from where much of the stairwell's light is borrowed.

The light comes in from floor-to-ceiling draperies that birdcage the room when they are (electronically) closed. When the drapes are closed, the room, and the stairway, has a more formal feeling to it, almost giving the whole top floor a ballroom effect.

LIGHTING A RICH, DARK SPACE

by Simon Davies, London West 8 Gallery

Swedish home dwellers are typically reticent about using colors in their spaces, particularly dark colors, and the understanding about how important lighting is to an interior is fairly new, says Simon Davies, lighting designer, interior designer, and co-owner of London West 8 Gallery in Stockholm, Sweden. "Our particular style is rather dark and rich and we work a great deal with lighting," says Davies. "Swedes are a practical people not much given over to extravagance, theater, or drama, but I am from London so there is a cross-cultural element here."

The apartment Davies designed—its walls and furnishings saturated in dark colors—is not uncommon in Sweden as much of the housing stock is from the turn of the century, but what is unusual are the rich colors he used. The ceilings in the apartment were kept white so that the space was dramatic, but not oppressive, and the crisp white woodwork helped to define spaces that would have been shapeless, says Davies.

But, there's nothing low-key about the lighting here. It's all planned accordingly to bring a theatrical flair to this 1890s apartment. Wherever one walks, there is an intense, dark aubergine-colored wall, or an eye-popping patterned floor, or eclectic furnishings and artwork that take center stage. To heighten the excitement, Davies uses his favorite lighting technique—taking a textured surface, or vignettes of sculptures, and lighting them very closely and intensely using spotlights with small 10-degree apertures from above. For instance, in tight situations, even in baths, Davies prefers to use exterior 12-volt halogen lights used in gardens because they are allowed indoors, are small, and the light is very directional and discreet. Most importantly, it helps Davies to create a spectacular setting where no ordinary lighting would ever do the trick.

DEEMPHASIZING LIGHT

The lamp on the ebony console is Bourgie by Ferrucio Laviani for Kartell. It's made out of a black-purple Plexiglas and has an extravagant, theatrical feel to it. Since the shade is dark, the lamp only throws light up and down, and does not add too strong a point of light on the other objects on the console.

DOWNLIGHTS

Davies rarely likes to use downlights to illuminate floors, but in this instance, he wanted to use the painted floor to reflect light back up into the space. Combining bounced light with the additional lighting on selected objects in the hallway created a moody, dramatic feeling to the entrance hall. "It's important that lighting is not placed too far away from walls, pictures, and the objects they are supposed to be lighting or else you get hopeless shadows and a very flat feel," says Davies. But the hallway is narrow enough that Davies was able to light it from side to side as well as centrally positioned downlighting. In addition, Davies placed a mirror against one end wall to give the impression of a doubled length of space. That meant it was important to use the downlights to create a long line of illumination that ran through the hallway, giving the eye a clear line to follow.

POINT OF LIGHT

"The lavender silk of the chair really needed to sing against the dark aubergine-colored matte walls," says Davies. To accomplish this, the chair is lit from above with a 50-watt quartz 70 lamp with a 10-degree spread on the beam. Davies says that this technique allows for very precise lighting effects and is something often ignored by most people when planning lighting schemes. "If you use a lamp with a very wide beam of light, the lux produced is much reduced," says Davies. "A tighter beam gets a dazzling amount of light onto an object."

OUTDOOR SPACES

Illuminating the outdoors is one of the most daunting challenges to tackle. The grounds seem limitless, the sky goes on forever, and there seem to be no boundaries in which to place fixtures. Then, there are tricks involving uplighting, downlighting, and questions: Where on or under a tree do we place a low-voltage spotlight so that the yard looks inviting? How do we light an entertainment or pool area so that it does not resemble the blinding light of a ball field? Then, the safety factor confuses us even more. When we add safety fixtures, we run the risk of overlighting the property, and, causing "light trespass" in which our illumination imposes itself onto our neighbor's yard. Yet, what do we do about our neighbor's yard—is there a way to use lighting techniques to literally "erase" their house from view at night?

In addition, there are several environmental conditions that should be considered when landscape lighting, such as coastal salt spray, desert heat, or the mountain snow and freeze factors. "Another factor which is becoming more and more of a concern is that of light glare and light trespass, and depending upon the population density and close proximity of others, these factors might have quite an impact." says landscape lighting designer Mark Carlson of Avalon Artistic Landscape Lighting. "Another problem is street lighting, commercial, and industrial lighting, as they can severely impact a landscape lighting layout due to their amount of spillover light."

To all of this, add in the burgeoning array of decorative outdoor fixtures. "The biggest mistake I see homeowners make when landscape lighting is in their use of inferior or improper products," adds Carlson. "Usually the homeowner goes to the local building supply center and buys a kit on the shelf. This can be a disaster because of the imposed limitations at the onset of the project." Carlson says that buying one kit off the shelf also limits the amount of different lighting effects that can be achieved through more thorough fixture selection. When faced with an overwhelming selection of fixtures and techniques, it's sometimes easier to stay with the path of least resistance and install walkway lights and spotlights that mimic the look of an airport landing strip. Only the right amount of fixtures and the layering of lighting techniques will do the most justice to the beauty of a landscape or sculpture garden at night.

A hand-built Japanese gate leads the way to this lush Northern California garden. Lighting designer Randall Whitehead, IALD, gave this entryway grace through simple illumination. A single candle invites visitors into a quiet sanctuary of light and shadow. Recessed low-voltage fixtures, tucked under the eaves, provide gentle plant illumination and pathway lighting.

AN OPTICAL ILLUSION

by Gus Wüstemann

It may sound counterintuitive, but architect Gus Wüstemann realized that the best way to light this balcony would be to eliminate any outdoor lighting. This Swiss house has a view over Lake Zurich to the South, and a view of the town and the horizon to the West, over which this balcony looks. But it took quite a bit of thought to figure out how to create an outdoor space that would feel as though it floated out over the town and yet have its edges seem like they melt into the horizon. The solution was to combine a transparent front railing, translucent side rails, and borrow light from the interior spaces to create an optical illusion.

There are no direct lighting sources on the balcony, there are no uplights, spotlights, downlights, and there are no portable lamps, either. The only lighting seen on the balcony comes from the glow spilling from the indoor illumination and into the outdoor space. "It's intentional that there are no direct lighting fixtures," says Wüstemann. "By eliminating fixtures, it allows the balcony's lines to slowly dissolve into the horizon." The rest of the lighting comes from below where the city's lights beam bright up to the hillside.

It took more than just installing a transparent front rail and eliminating lights to create the effect. To begin, there are two transparent walls to the balcony. One wall separates the interior but leads out to the balcony. By creating a separate box with a transparent wall, Wüstemann was able to begin the visual process of creating depth that gives the feeling that the front of the balcony is actually dissolving into the horizon. It's a simple trick of the eye, but one that only a master of lighting design and material use, such as Wüstemann, could pull off.

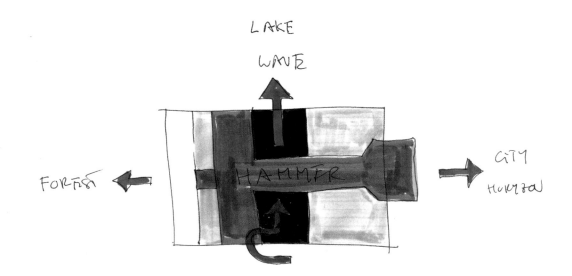

The balcony is the handle part of the hammer shape that extends from the interior of the apartment to the exterior. Wüstemann explains, "It was important to make it look like the balcony, or the hammer, was shooting out of the roof and into the horizon, and this was technically the most difficult part of the project."

Spilled Lighting

The glowing railing on the side of the balcony beyond the first glass partition comes from a series of fluorescent light fixtures placed behind the translucent Skobalit panels. The top of the lit railing is made of copper for durability, then painted in the same color as the raw MDF used on other parts of the balcony.

Floor

The floor of the balcony reflects spilled and natural light because it is glossy. It's created from layers of epoxy and fiberglass that was laid over a base of multiplex wooden board. The epoxy and fiberglass floor was then painted to match the MDF surface of the structure, which Wüstemann calls "the hammer."

Railing

The transparent glass front railing reflects the sparkle of city lights, spilled interior light, and natural light from the stars and moon. In addition, the glass lets light pass through its surface. The glass sits on solid wood and is reinforced in the front with a hidden steel frame. "The glass sits frameless at the fringe of the hammer, so it appears as if the sculpture disappears into the horizon," explains Wüstemann.

AN OUTDOOR DESTINATION

by Janet Lennox Moyer

TOP AND ABOVE: Lighting creates a dramatic difference at night in this seating area in the farthest area of this property. During the day, another neighbor's house can be seen through the top of the arbor, but at night, Moyer used lighting to erase it. "To fully feel that this is the farthest point from the house, I needed to make it appear far away," says Moyer. She focused the nighttime lighting on the dining table and the arbor columns. The six fixtures on the arbor roof appear like little stars as they erase the roof and everything above it. The outer four fixtures are used to softly light the table and the inner two fixtures focus on the centerpieces during dining.

Landscape lighting takes on another layer when there's sculpture on the property that begs to be properly illuminated. This northern California home, with a landscape designed by Valerie Matzger, and outdoor lighting designed by Janet Lennox Moyer, had other challenges that lighting would contend with, as well. "We had to erase the view of a neighbor's house by locating light in strategic areas," says Moyer. "In other places on the property, we created visual walls by creating a sense of boundaries with light."

Because this was the second time Moyer worked with the family, she knew how they felt about light. "They had a good understanding of how lighting can complement what other designers have done, especially at night," says Moyer, also the author of *The Landscape Lighting Book*. She says that most homeowners make the mistake of overlighting outdoor areas, which translates into using too many sources of light that can be seen with the eye. "If you can see the lamp in the fixture, you will have glare. The starting point of any good landscape lighting plan is the decision to hide the light source." She points out that lighting needs to be cohesive to create a visually stable outdoor scene because with too much glare and too much contrast, the eye will want to dart around the yard and then easily tire.

That's exactly how she approached this home's landscape lighting plan. "It doesn't take much light to create visual destinations or to highlight a wall," she says. Since it's northern California, the family wanted the property to be lit for outdoor living, as well. Moyer's plan was to let the lighting help *reveal* the elements that comprise the outdoor living spaces, which included a number of sculptures throughout the property.

Spot on Pot

The downlights are mounted above the bow window and aimed onto the planting outside to provide a sense of depth into the garden from inside the living room. Moyer created a visual destination at the end of the pathway by focusing some of the downlights onto the pot. During the day, the red pot recedes into the foliage, but at night, it comes alive because of a spot from the eaves that is angled toward the piece of art.

Pathway Lighting

The pathway that leads to the back of the garden is lit with only a couple of layers of lighting. The main layer of light on the path comes from the uplighting on the orange-blossomed Brugmansia plants. Though there are some shadows cast on the walk, the path is clearly delineated. The path is further illuminated by the downlighting coming from the eaves of the house. The eaves' downlighting—which are surface-mounted MR-11 and MR-16 fixtures with low-voltage 20 watt lamps—are actually aimed at the plantings, letting some of the illumination spill onto the path. This creates the fill light on that path that mingles with the uplighting from the plants. The variations in brightness create a comfortable, balanced, and most of all, inviting pathway into the garden.

Moyer revealed the living areas by creating destination scenes with lighting. She encourages clients, such as this one, to only use light when and where they need it so all of the lighting does not go on automatically at night. Moyer used several Lutron Grafik Eye multiple-scene controllers connected together to to create up to sixteen scenes between the back and front of the property. That way, if the homeowners are entertaining in one dining spot, they don't have to turn on the lights in areas not being used that evening.

But there are many times the family entertains indoors, and they want to be able to see the outdoor art during the nighttime. This requires a fine balance of light to be able to view the outdoors from the indoors. The reason is that glare from interior lighting can create reflections of the inside room (including furnishings) on windows, and it becomes too difficult to see what is going on outdoors. Moyer says the challenge of being able to see the outdoors clearly from indoors at night is simple. "The basic rule is that in order to not have the interior reflect on the inside window, make sure that it's brighter indoors than it is outdoors," she explains.

ERASED VIEW

During the day, the neighbor's house can be seen from the dining space. At night, the correct positioning, aiming, and shielding of landscape lighting completely erases the neighbor's house. Moyer says that it is easy to achieve this kind of effect by keeping light away from the undesirable things that you can see in a space, and putting light onto elements that you want to be revealed after dark. The space feels intimate when it's lit at night, even though the "walls" making this outside dining room light up. "Having the boundaries of a space lit helps the space feel more comfortable since it allows us to see the boundary," Moyer explains. All the downlighting on the table and the floor of this dining area is coming from small MR-11 low-voltage fixtures tucked into the branches of a mature tree that overhangs the patio area. When the branches are not large enough for a "mounting canopy," Moyer has used ring-mount "hanging" fixtures, which will sway with the breeze. Some of the fixtures are located above the lower branches, which is what creates the soft patterns on the table and on the floor.

TRELLIS AND SCULPTURE

Along the top of the trellis Moyer placed a series of small MR-11 low-voltage downlights that wash gently over the columns and onto the steps. Through the trellis is a sculpture of a man that is the brightest lit object in this scene, serving as both primary focal point in the distance and visual destination, helping lead people to the next room of this garden. The trellis lighting acts as a frame surrounding the piece of sculpture, but it does not cause too much contrast, making it comfortable on the eyes when dining at the table during the night hours. Moyer lit the planting behind the sculpture to provide depth. Then, she added a softer layer of light on the two sides of the garden between the sculpture and the trellis. This provides "visual transportation" between the sculpture and the foreground to make the scene visually stable.

VISUAL WALLS

Moyer used lighting to create a sense of boundaries around the mosaic dining table. "This visual boundary helps people feel comfortable in the space," she says. Moyer created illuminated "walls" by surrounding the scene with up- and downlighting amongst the foliage around the table. The downlighting, in the trees, also hits the top of the dining table and brings out the mosaic artwork, even at night. There are a lot of lights used in the foliage, she says, but no light sources are visible.

As she did with this home's lighting plan, Moyer explains that exterior scenes are typically up to the brightness of ½-foot to 5-foot candles, and interiors are lit to have the brightness of 10- to 20-foot candles. This requires the family to bring the exterior lighting levels up, and turn the interior levels down when they entertain outdoors. That's the benefit of planning "zones" of lighting which can be dimmed separately through a multi-scene lighting system.

Lighting sculpture demands planning, as well. "A sculpture will tell you how to light it," says Moyer. "But you can't really light a piece of sculpture correctly until it's in place in the garden." Moyer usually brings power to a location where a piece of art will sit, and then works on the lighting after it has settled in.

Moyer borrows stage-lighting techniques to light sculpture, but only if the art represents an animal or a person. She lights up one to two sides of the piece, 35 to 45 degrees off dead center of the nose. "By doing this, you get the natural form of the person depicted, and you don't get the scary shadows created from straight up or down lighting," Moyer explains.

ABOVE: The other side of the trellis is a set of half-circular steps leading out to the sculpture of the man. The steps are lit from the lights coming off of the top of the trellis, and by the uplighting in the surrounding foliage. Moyer aimed these lights to highlight the steps for safety, but not to create any harsh light on people as they walk up or down the stairs. She has carefully aimed them so that no one can see into the fixtures and be hit by the bright light. This is achieved by a combination of aiming angle (which needs to be as close to straight down as possible and always less than 35 degrees), selecting a fixture with the lamp regressed into the housing of the fixture, and then using a 45-degree honeycomb louver. The stair area is evenly lit not only to make sure that they are visible and safe, but to show the clever planting of moss in between the stairs.

SCULPTURE

The outstretched arm of the man, which is also a fountain from which water drips, is the most important element of this particular sculpture. During the day, dappled sunlight highlights the man, while at night his form is in full view with the use of ground recessed, fully sealed uplights (this type of sealed fixture is referred to as a direct-burial fixture in the lighting industry, and Moyer only uses this type of below-grade fixture—never an open fixture called a "well-light." This is because the ground is the most corrosive environment and it is difficult to keep below grade fixtures functioning). Each of the five below-grade fixtures, placed all the way around the sculpture in order to show his form, no matter what direction someone views him, utilizes only 20 watts to create the lighting effect. There's uplighting in the shrubbery and redwood tree, plus downlighting from within the tree to gently illuminate the sculpture's surroundings and to eliminate too much contrast. The framework of the lighting plan for this sculpture makes him look welcoming, not alone and foreboding.

PATHWAY AND COLUMNS

In the distance, there's a distinctive view of the four columns of the farthest arbor, but there is not too much contrast when looking down the path from the sculpture. In fact, the balance of light from the sculpture down to the arbor makes the red brick path look welcoming and safe, not far away or frightening to walk down. The pathway to the arbor is indirectly lit by uplighting the rose obelisks. This vertical lighting between the upper area and the lower patio visually connects the two, making the walk feel safe and comfortable.

IN FOCUS

AN ESSENTIAL LIGHTING TOOL

Computerized renderings breathe life into outdoor lighting plans…even before the plans are in place. Lighting designer Janet Lennox Moyer, author of *The Landscape Lighting Book*, has wanted to be able to show clients a realistic image of their potential lighting for all of her thirty years practicing lighting design. While working with photographer George Gruel, the opportunity finally arrived. He created a rendering process utilizing his talents as a fine artist and the program Photoshop on his Macintosh computer. Starting with a daytime photo or a digitized rendering of a client's garden, Moyer would describe the lighting techniques and effects she wanted to incorporate in the garden. Gruel would create a darkened nighttime version of the garden space. Today his technique is finessed; he paints in Photoshop, but not with the lighting tool. He layers brush-strokes of light to reveal form and elements building the light composition. This form of visualization helps clients understand what their landscape lighting will look like. "Clients have a hard time understanding what lighting can do for their property," says Moyer. "Until now, the only real way to show someone what lighting could do was to set up a mockup in their garden. While still more effective than renderings, the mockup process is far more intense, which translates into being more expensive." The beauty of renderings is that they appear like photos of the finished project. And, as Moyer says, they are very realistic. "When you show a client a rendering, that's how they expect it to be once it's finished, and with this process, it always works."

This rendering of a spa in Northern California helped the clients understand how low-voltage lighting during the nighttime would create a private space for them to enjoy from the tub or chairs on the patio. The lighting gives both sculptures a subtle glow and reveals selected elements surrounding the spa. Uplighting of tree ferns in the distance gives a little depth to the scene. Uplighting the Japanese Maples and the Palm trees provides a framework around the garden. Downlighting onto the dwarf red Maple provides cohesion around the spa and provides safety by light spilling onto the adjacent stairs. In addition, Moyer was able to show the client how a small bit of uplighting would cast a glow on the Japanese maple and the stone area near the chairs.

THE FLOW OF LIGHT

by Ron Yeo, FAIA

Can an architect and his client work together to design a lighting plan, especially when it comes to the sometimes complicated task of landscape lighting? Client Ron Quon of Corona del Mar, California, proved that it can indeed be done with spectacular results. He tackled the task of planning the lighting for his new home alongside architect Ron Yeo. Although most homeowners would not have the time, guts, or talent to design the lighting system on their own—especially outdoor lighting—Quon took on the challenge of investigating, observing, and analyzing lighting for his own home. As a result, the front exterior courtyard glows like a guiding light that invites guests to come and explore the house.

From the beginning of the project, the client's design goals included a wind-protected courtyard that would serve as a transition from street entry using a meandering stream with cascading waterfalls that flow into a tranquil pond. Quon says lighting played a key role in designing this courtyard, "The intent was to use lighting to lead visitors from the gate entry through the inner courtyard to the front door, then use lights to initially illuminate the courtyard landscape, then focus the lighting on the artwork in the alcoves in the hallways, and then use lighting to finally see the interior of the great room through the courtyard entry door."

Quon researched lighting by visiting completed homes and showrooms and reviewing websites to learn what type of lighting creates a dazzling landscape. After doing this research Quon decided that systems using MR-16 lamps would be ideal. Quon liked the ability to change wattage bulbs when he wanted little or more intensity, and they can be mounted for straight-on lighting or for more focused lighting. "To control lighting, we piled rocks in front of the glass lenses or buried them deeper in the rock bed," he says. "This way, we could control the amount of lighting for each area rather than use a dimmer that would affect all of the lights."

ABOVE: The landscape lighting consists mainly of uplights placed at plant and boulder locations as well as in the stream. To highlight the stream, waterfalls, and ponds, low-voltage submersible halogens were installed directly in the water. The flow of water over the lights adds a subtle shimmer to the landscape and makes everything come alive at night.

RIGHT: The plan shows how the interior wraps around the terrace/deck, providing spilled light. The courtyard terrace is illuminated from above from the 6-foot [1.8 m] roof overhang and the glow from the interior lights through the glass walls. Yeo believes that landscape lighting and interior lighting should work hand in hand.

LIGHTING GOAL

The homeowner's goal was to create a courtyard that would be a main focus and gathering point from the street, as well as from the interior rooms that wrap around it. To achieve this goal, the homeowner researched lighting. He photographed ideas and concepts that he liked and then downloaded them into an Excel file. "Placing photos on the computer was a great way to review and discuss items with my wife," says Quon. "Then, I'd communicate the research and ideas to Yeo." The results of his research: MR-16 lamps as the lighting foundation throughout.

GLASS PANES

The floor-to-ceiling glass panes are clear glass without any tints or films to color or reflect interior ambient lights. When the interior lighting is set at a more intense level, it makes the glass completely transparent from the exterior.

HIDDEN LIGHTS

Though the seating area of the courtyard looks bright and inviting, there are no portable fixtures creating the illumination, and there is a minimum of exterior architectural lighting around the table as well. "I feel that the source of light should not be apparent unless it is treated as an interesting art form, such as a hanging fixture or sconce," says Yeo. "That's why the seating area of the courtyard borrows interior light with just a few recessed fixtures over the entryway for extra brightness." The lighting plan of this space emphasizes the Zen quality, the simplicity, and the openness of the courtyard and interior without inviting any clutter into view.

A PLAY OF LIGHT AND SHADOWS

by Mark Carlson, Avalon Artistic Landscape Lighting

"My favorite landscape lighting technique is probably silhouetting, or shadow lighting. I love how light plays through plant material or a structural element," says Mark Carlson, lighting designer of Avalon Artistic Landscape Lighting. "It's the play of light and shadow that makes an outdoor area come alive." Nowhere is that more evident than in the lighting plan Carlson created for this property that was landscaped by designer Michael Glassman.

"Based upon the placement of a fixture, you can silhouette the form against a wall washed with light or maybe create crisp shadows that are thrown onto a wall when the form is front lit," Carlson adds. The effects begin at the entry courtyard of this house in California. A fountain became the focal point, especially when it was illuminated and the lights created several light and shadowing effects.

The water feature could be viewed from several areas in the courtyard, and Carlson said he was fortunate enough to have a large wall behind it to work with to create the interplay of light and shadows. "As the water splashed into the basin from the bowl above, it caused a dancing effect of light onto the wall—it was spectacular," says Carlson. "Overall, it took five lights to create the dramatic look, but the impact from this element and the amount of indirect lighting given to the entry walk was a perfect way to greet guests."

Carlson says that once there are long rows of trees, or an extra long pool, then there are different approaches to take in what to light and how much to light. "I will always apply light based upon what the client wants and what level of light they appreciate," he says. "I try to illuminate enough trees to create a rhythm and theme across the setting." But, he says, the more features and trees that are uplit, the more the place or setting will be impacted by the light. The reason that so many lights were used for this pool setting is because this particular client enjoyed entertaining and was looking for more visual impact and drama around the pool and in the front courtyard.

LEFT: Lighting can throw shadows onto a wall behind the plant material. These flowers, in the front courtyard, created a lot of interest by casting subtle shadows on the wall. "The light bounced off the walls to give indirect lighting to the entry walk," says Carlson. "To create this effect you should work with plant material that is somewhat airy and open in nature, thereby allowing light to pass through onto the wall behind."

Spots

Carlson placed two spotlights in the planter beneath the water feature and aimed them to shine onto the potted citrus trees flanking the fountain. This lighting technique threw shadows from the citrus trees onto the wall behind the fountain.

Washer

To add to the drama around the fountain, Carlson placed a washer light directly behind the feature next to the wall. The fixture washed light directly up the wall to help silhouette part of the fountain. "It gave the effect of the sun rising from behind the fountain," says Carlson.

Uplights

There were multiple effects created with lighting. "We caused shadow play from the uplights below the feature inside the water basin that created the shadows above and on the wall," says Carlson. "What was interesting, and unintentional, is that these shadows came together to create an outline of a flame at the tip of the feature."

LEFT: Two downlights hidden overhead in the patio cover lights up the second tiered fountain on the property. The two fixtures crosslight the feature, which is the best way to illuminate this type of water fountain. "Most of the time you will see a tiered fountain lit only from below at ground level—what ends up happening is that the underside of the bowls are lit and shadow remains on top of each level," says Carlson. "Another good way to light a fountain is by using a combination of both down- and uplights to highlight the features."

BELOW: The palm trees behind the pool are uplit. The pool is lit from within using all standard high-voltage fixtures provided by the pool contractor. The standard pool lights add color to the water and give a soothing glow to the overall setting. The pergola structures provide the areas with the downlighting, and uplights are used to accent various palm trees.

OPPOSITE: A single uplight in the planter behind the table is aimed to wash the corner patio walls with light. This simple technique silhouettes the table and the miniature tree in the pot. Just one uplight adds a lot of drama to this corner because the light's glow comes indirectly through the table and chairs ironwork.

A SUBTLE BEACON OF LIGHT

by Kanner Architects

So much of the interior lighting of this 25-foot (7.6 m) -wide contemporary glass house in California spills outdoors that not many outdoor fixtures were needed. In addition, the site itself has a strong natural light by virtue of its perch on a hill in the Santa Monica Mountains. "Because of its altitude, the house receives light from all sides during the majority of the day," says Stephen Kanner of Kanner Architects. "The house is also high enough so that it is unaffected by marine layer, which can darken the sky." Marine layer, a cool, moist, sometimes fog-laden layer of air caused by the cooling effect of the Pacific Ocean, can sometimes bring a veil of dimness into an otherwise light, bright house near the water.

Oftentimes, as it is with a house with water in the distance or nearby, connecting the indoors and the outdoors is essential for year-round enjoyment of weather. The interior and exterior lights of this house work together by connecting both spaces at night. "Walls of glass—some operable—let the indoor and outdoor spaces

During dusk, the first floor of the interior of the house has a lower level of light than the exterior, and that is why the reflection of the landscape is so prevalent on the front window of the lower half of the house. The lighting level of the upstairs interior is brighter than the outside, which is why there is no reflection of the landscape on the upper windows. The windows did not have the need for tinting because the numerous architectural projections naturally provide a shade for the glass.

come together to increase spaces and make the house feel and look physically larger," says Kanner. "At the same time, the whole house opens itself up and welcomes and participates in its environment."

One of the issues of connecting glass-wrapped spaces is about how to illuminate the house so you can see to the outside clearly and to the inside just as clearly without creating shadows, confusing reflections, or glare. "To create a two-way perspective between outside and inside, the interior needs to be lit more brightly than the outside or kept to the same light level as the outside," says Kanner. "Whichever side of the glass is dimmer will be less visible from the other side." By keeping the lighting levels of the interior and exterior of this house the same, the views inside and out are crystal clear at night.

Only the entry points of the back of the house are lit because this is the public face of the house. "While the house, overall, is designed to stand out in its environment, it is designed to do so only during the day," says Kanner. "We wanted it to better blend in at night and not be a shining beacon of difference." To create a subtly illuminated rock garden, the placement of the lights, windows, glass walls, and rocks were all carefully choreographed so the stones would be best highlighted.

Slotted Window

The lighted, slot-shaped window glowing in the second story volume of the living room lets in natural light during the day. At night, it has a magical visual effect of a candle when the interior is lit from within.

Pavers

A standard in-ground uplight was installed in the front courtyard pavers. The uplight sends a pool of light up under the entryway roofline.

Entry Door

The front entryway has one recessed can light directly over the entry door. "We chose to use light from inside the house to illuminate the courtyard through glass walls, which eliminated the use for more fixtures," says Kanner.

Soffits

The downlights installed on the soffits help guide guests to the entryway of the house. The remaining lighting from the interior provides a welcome to the visitor and provides enough light to entertain in the front courtyard.

TECHNIQUES OF THE TRADE

by Mark Carlson, Avalon Artistic Landscape Lighting

OVERHEAD EFFECTS
Three fixtures give this curved vine-covered patio its
sparkling overhead lighting effects. The fixtures are spaced
between the overhead arched members to create the interplay of light and shadow. "We only located fixtures to one side
of the structure," says Mark Carlson of Avalon Artistic
Landscape Lighting. Two other fixtures were placed along the
back of the arches to shed light on the Japanese maple that
is set up against the wall. A decorative hanging fixture and
candle arrangement further illuminates the table surface.

ABOVE: SAFE SURFACE LIGHTING
This hidden terrace garden was lit up enough to ensure a
safe transition between different elevation changes. In addition to safety, the lighting illuminates the varied elements—
such as sculpture and topiaries—within this space. The large
Japanese maple tree and the nearby larger oak tree were uplit from below. An additional uplight in the far back grazes an
iron work fence and sprinkles light onto another large oak
tree behind the fencing giving even more depth to this space.
The remaining three fixtures are all downlights casting illumination streaming out of the oak trees. "We used the downlights on the oak trees to light up the terrace stones, topiary,
and sculptures," explains Carlson.

RIGHT: HIGHLIGHTING TEXTURE
The lighting shows the texture of the stonework bridge.
Grazing light across the surface of the bridge brings out the
shadows created by the stonework. "The closer you are to the
surface, the more dramatic the shadow-play of light," says
Carlson. There's a total of six lights in this scene: Two uplights behind the bridge are directed onto the willow and the
oak trees. Two other lights are set up to graze the outer sides
of the bridge. The last two lights are angled from planter
beds in front of the bridge opening, to graze the ends of the
bridge, and to spill onto the stone walk.

ABOVE: CREATING ILLUSION OF CANDLE GLOW
This metal bird within a cage is lit with artificial lighting, but it appears as though the candles are creating the glow. "We took a small hanging light, secured it to the top of the cage and hid the small gauge of wire down along the metal cage material," explains Carlson. "This technique casts a soft light down onto the bird and flower arrangement, but when the candles are lit, they give the illusion of lighting the bird."

LEFT: POOLS OF LIGHT
"There is so much to enjoy visually from the play of light glowing within the pond, water gently dripping off the metal sculpture, and the reflections of light glowing on the rear walls," says Carlson. A total of eight fixtures were used in this scene, five of which are underwater lights. The underwater lights are set within a foot (0.3 m) of the waterline and under the rock ledge around the pond's perimeter. This special niche recess under the ledge allowed Carlson to hide the fixtures so the glow reaches out into the pond. To add to the drama, two underwater stone sculpture pieces are lit for an added surprise to the pond. The other lights include two soft washing lights that graze the walls and a small stone sculpture of a man holding an umbrella. The last light is used behind the doors to create a glow that is seen against the backside of the glass panels.

COMPLETE DWELLINGS

Many of us may not give much thought to how an entire house is lit. Only when we realize it's too dark or too bright inside or out, do we notice lighting. "You can't think of lighting as only lighting," says architect Rand Elliott. "It's a central idea that's important on any project. The most important thing about lighting is that you need a concept before you start." One rule of thumb he suggests is that each room should have light and dark spaces to give the feeling of a rich experience as you move through the house.

The responsibility to choose lighting fixtures and techniques to control each layer for an entire dwelling is overwhelming. However, when it's fully integrated throughout, the results are simple and gratifying—with the push of a button, you change the lights in an entire house.

In the following pages, you'll see how various designers and architects pulled an entire lighting concept through a house or apartment, even when restrictions caused problems. The lighting plan of one modern glass house not only highlights the craggy natural landscape surrounding the dwelling, but also helped the whole house to be nearly invisible from the street during the daytime and the nighttime.

Another project in Switzerland entailed rebuilding a claustrophobic loft space in the attic of a house and using light—in the form of concealed fluorescent lights—to brighten up the dark space.

Lighting can create or dismiss the overall feeling in a home. The proper lighting in a renovated California desert home with strong collections of artwork, rich, vivid colors, and angular architecture, provided a soft cohesion. In another project, the almost exclusive use of recessed fixtures used throughout the space seems to have visually enlarged the long, narrow Manhattan loft. Lighting, as you will witness, can fix everything, or nothing at all.

The design objective of this contemporary home, designed by Kanner architects, was to blur the line between the inside and outside while taking advantage of the brilliant sunlight and cool breezes of Southern California's Pacific Palisades. At night, the crisp light that fills the glass-clad interior of the modernist home spills outside to illuminate the wide patio that is used for entertaining, providing an indoor-outdoor link. Ground uplights and a lit water element enhance the exterior illumination.

STRETCHING SPACE WITH LIGHT

by Abigail Shachat, AJS Design

"It takes a lot of downlights to create a well-lit room," says Abigail Shachat, principal and architect of AJS Design in New York City. "Most people underlight a home, overemphasize parts of a space with poorly placed lighting, or place too few downlights too far apart, which create arcs of light on the wall." Though it took a lot of downlights to illuminate this West Village loft, Shachat used each fixture as part of an architectural strategy to stretch the space.

The loft Shachat designed was typical of many urban lofts: it was long and narrow and all the windows were at one end of the space. A wall down the middle of the space made things worse by creating a 30-foot (9.1 m)-long bowling-alley effect. Though there's much that architectural renovating can achieve to fix the space, Shachat knew that lighting could enhance the feeling that the space was wider than it actually was.

The concept is to use lighting to carry the eye from one room to another, "This way, the lines of the space were extended. In a New York City apartment, often you only get light from one direction, so you need to bring light in from other directions," Shachat says as she explains how she allows the light from one room to "inform" an adjacent space to create a greater sense of depth. "In this loft, for instance, when the homeowner switches on lights at the same time in the living and master bedroom, the living room actually feels wider since the two lit up rooms are connected," she says.

One way to work with lighting is to use layers of recessed fixtures (as Shachat did here using products from Cooper Industries) with various lamp types to create different effects throughout the loft. Shachat used a combination of A-lamps for a softer wall washing effect, PAR lamps for stronger downlights, such as those over the dining table, and MR-16 lamps for accent lighting. Her layered approach bolsters the architecture rather than overwhelms it. "Many designers overdramatize space allowing lighting to emphasize too much at the same level of illumination," she says. "I like to use lighting in more of a supporting role. When lighting is done well you should not really notice it, you should just notice the space."

But it's not always an easy fix to use recessed lighting in urban dwellings. "The biggest problem in most apartments is that there are constraints imposed by the limits of a building, such as concrete slab ceilings, that prevent the use of recessed lighting," says Shachat. Luckily, this loft already had drywall ceilings so she had many choices in the types of fixtures she used and where they could be placed.

CORNER LIGHT

To illuminate the corner of the wall that separates the entry from the kitchen, Shachat designed a type of built-in vertical lamp. She designed the light using acrylic Light Blocks covering a PAR lamp used inside the corner. "This light takes the place of an entry table lamp," says Shachat. "Integrally tinted plaster in dark blue frames the light to create a focal point of architectural interest as soon as the homeowners enter the loft."

DINING ROOM LIGHTING

Shachat didn't use a pendant over the dining table because she did not want to create an extra visual layer between the kitchen and dining room. "It wasn't necessary to anchor the dining area with a pendant, and it would have been too visually active," she says. Instead, she used one of her favorite lighting techniques to illuminate the dining area. To best light a dining room table, Shachat prefers to use three points of light, as she did here. For an average 6-foot (1.8 meter) -long table, Shachat likes to put a recessed spot in the center that can be turned on before and after dinner. Two other downlights flank the side of the center spot, and they are meant to be turned on while serving and eating dinner.

ABOVE: A walnut wall divider in the main living area frames a desk and storage wall. "No one wants to go back into a vacuum to do work," says Shachat. The desk here became part of the main space, and the floating ceiling above the desk anchors and defines the area by creating a second ceiling. Two recessed lights in the floating ceiling give general illumination over the desk.

LEFT: An entire back wall of storage could easily overwhelm a space if the right lighting was not used. Here, the line of recessed ceiling lighting is meant to create a sense of flow down the long corridor while it frames the light coming from the window. The slot of light at the top of the bookcase reinforces the idea of the ceiling as a floating plane that the storage units recede behind. Shachat placed a strip of halogen lights from Ardee into the slot to emphasize this effect.

Shachat had a four-prong plan to light the loft. First, she lit the perimeter of the apartment with wall washers for an overall glow. Then, she created "lit zones," which accented specific areas with downlighting, such as the dining and living spaces. Within the zones, Shachat added accent lighting to focus on features, such as the walnut room divider and its perforated sliding stainless steel door, the fireplace in the living room, and the other distinctive materials used in the loft. Finally, floor and table lamps were added to create intimacy by bringing the light down to a human scale.

Island Pendants

The mercury glass pendants from Ameico are incandescent R-lamps. "The fixtures push the light down instead of out," explains Shachat. She placed them low enough over the island so the lamp is hidden, but high enough so they don't hit her client's head. "There's no real rule of thumb about how high to hang pendants," she says. "I'm always adjusting the height of fixtures in the field."

Back splash Lighting

Stainless steel back splashes are difficult to light well, says Shachat. "Because they are so reflective the surface becomes extremely active once lit," she says. The halogen lighting used under the cabinet reflects off of the stainless steel back splash. "The under-cabinet fixtures are halogen. Under-cabinet fixtures that face away from the back splash make the cavity come alive," says Shachat. "If the fixtures faced toward the back splash, the surface would look even more active."

"You can create a variety of lighting experiences with recessed downlighting and not have the fixtures look so evident," says Shachat. Although many downlights may all look alike, Shachat points out that the internal engineering of various fixtures produced by different manufacturers allow for distinctive effects. "Outwardly all the fixtures will look the same but internally they will be engineered to produce different results," she explains. In addition, the more expensive fixtures create a simple, more unified look, because, for instance, a fixture can be flangeless to create a cleaner ceiling plane.

Lighting this loft with recessed lighting kept the vertical planes clean and the horizontal surfaces simple. "Lighting can make or break a job," says Shachat. "If lighting is well done, you don't notice the lighting—all you really notice is how good the room feels."

Lighting a television wall is easier than most people think. "When a TV wall has other elements on it, such as a fireplace, I always put a light over the television on a separate switch," says Shachat.

A HOUSE WITH A LIGHT TOUCH

by Randall Whitehead Lighting Design, Inc.

Lighting can make or break the overall feeling desired in a home. If it weren't for the proper lighting in this renovated California desert home, the strong collections of artwork, vivid colors, and angular architecture would have an overwhelming effect on not only the homeowners, but on the guests, as well. It was the job of veteran lighting designer, Randall Whitehead, to make sure that the homeowner and his guests would feel welcomed, and not overpowered, by the sumptuous interior design. Working together with Jonathan Hopp of Jonathan Hopp Interior Design, Whitehead's addition of an inviting layer of ambient lighting throughout the house created the right balance.

RIGHT: A glimpse of the dining room can be seen from the opening that leads into the kitchen. Recessed adjustable low-voltage fixtures offer illumination for the African sculpture and abstract painting.

PROPER LIGHTING FOR FABRICS

The textures of the fabrics are brought out in both daylight and night light. The recessed fixtures use halogen sources to provide a quality of light that is whiter than standard incandescent sources. Since halogen is an incandescent source, it can have the same amber glow as standard incandescent sources when dimmed to a more intimate level of illumination.

PICTURE-WINDOW EFFECTS

Fabrics were chosen not only for durability, but to withstand the strong light of the desert sun coming in through the picture windows. The window coverings were kept to a minimum to let a generous amount of natural light inside, and to allow the subtly exterior landscape lighting to draw guests outside at night.

FIREPLACE DIVIDER WALL

A large fireplace wall divides the living and dining room areas. Recessed, adjustable, low-voltage fixtures illuminate the Japanese screen and the raku vessels in the niches above the piano on the left. A linear indirect fixture using a long-life Xenon source is mounted on top of the room divider to create additional ambient light because it bounces off of the ceiling and into the rest of the room. Since the fireplace is massive, the sconces that flank the screen had to be in scale. "The 30-inch (76 cm)-tall fixtures were standard-issue products, but they were finished with a high-heat paint that matches the wall color," says Whitehead. "This way they became less decorative and more architectural."

Enhanced Wood Cabinets

To bring out the grain in the oil-rubbed finished wood cabinets, Whitehead installed low-voltage recessed fixtures to give the cabinetry a wash of light. Lighting hidden below offers good shadowless task light along the counter top.

Hanging Pendant

The accordion-type pendant light fixture, called Zoom by Serien, hangs above the breakfast table. The fixture, made of steel and a translucent foil, can be made larger or smaller simply by pulling it apart or squeezing it together. There is a series of halogen bulbs built into each of the fixture's metal slats, and when the fixture is lit up, the bulbs look like Christmas lights, says Whitehead.

Under-Cabinet Lighting

Conventional under-cabinet lighting would not work well with the highly polished granite countertop because the homeowner would be able to see a distracting mirror image of the light in the secular surface. Instead, Whitehead used an under cabinet linear task light with an L-bracket option to shield the light source from the countertops and redirect the illumination towards the back splash, which would in turn bounce it down onto the countertop. By using this approach, the lighting was hidden, and glare and reflection eliminated without compromising the quality and quantity of illumination.

This Palm Springs home, built in 1968, had all the great bones of mid-century classic architecture, but the homeowner felt it needed updating. What pulls all the new—and older—design elements together is the extensive interior and exterior lighting plan. Whitehead believes there are three elements within each space that need to be lighted: art, architecture, and people. In this house, all three were present throughout every inch of the home.

"If homeowners only used accent lighting, which is something I see all the time, the room would have a "museum effect" which subtly tells family and friends that the art is more important than they are," says Whitehead. "Think about lighting the people in a home first because you must humanize the light." He explains that a layer of ambient light softens the shadows on people's faces as well as the hard edges of the 1960s architecture.

Still another twist to the lighting plan that Whitehead needed to contend with was the actual desert light. Use of darker colors and finishes in this house dramatically differ from what is typically used in homes in hot climates. Granite countertops are offset by mahogany cabinetry, various-colored tile is use in the master bathroom, the powder room is set against a wall of chocolate red tiles, and the terrazzo tile was replaced with dark slate floors.

ABOVE RIGHT: The master bath has a serene Japanese feeling, and it's filled with warm muted colors. Two pairs of "Stripes" wall sconces by Boyd Lighting provide task light at the two sinks. A single recessed adjustable low-voltage fixture illuminates the large raku vessel on the counter. Outside, the low-voltage accent lights cast painterly shadows on the frosted glass surround of the walk-in shower.

BELOW RIGHT: In the backyard, which faces a ridge of mountains, stands a modern red metal sculpture sitting atop a low water feature. Exterior, adjustable, low-voltage fixtures by BK Lighting illuminate the sculpture and the fountain, while additional ground-mounted, adjustable, low-voltage fixtures highlight the palm trees beyond.

OPPOSITE PAGE TOP: The living room is large, so Whitehead used a series of recessed, adjustable, low-voltage fixtures to define space by creating inviting islands of illumination. Since the living room is oversized, low-voltage, linear, indirect fixtures were mounted on top of the clerestory windows to add much-needed ambient lighting.

TRANSLUCENT GLASS

The translucent doors are back-illuminated with low-voltage, recessed fixtures to create an inviting glow that just naturally leads people to the entry. In essence, the doors take the place of traditional side-mounted lanterns.

LIGHTED PLANTINGS

Mature cacti and succulents were added to the existing palm trees to help draw the eye to the horizontal lines of the building. Low-voltage, directional fixtures by BK Lighting were installed to bring out the sculptural quality of the plantings. Color-corrected, daylight, blue filters were used in the fixtures to create a whiter light to enhance the color of the plantings.

LEFT: The powder room packs a lot of drama into a compact space. A pair of textured glass sconces flanks the sink while recessed, adjustable, low-voltage fixtures punch up the stone basin and the modern interpretation of a Macintosh chair.

HANGING PENDANT

The tall ceilings made the room feel uninviting, so Whitehead chose to hang a large Ingo Maurer paper pendant to float above the dining table. "By using an overscale fixture it created a secondary ceiling line to help humanize the space, and the glowing material helps to offset the actual size of the pendant," Whitehead explains. "This fixture uses dimmable screw-in compact fluorescent bulbs that are very energy efficient, and they cut down on the output of heat that would be generated from conventional incandescent bulbs. This is big news in the desert." The pendant uses five 16-watt compact fluorescent lamps that give off the same amount of warm illumination as would five 75-watt incandescent bulbs.

UPLIT GLASS SCULPTURE

The homeowner has a large collection of art glass, one piece of which stands in the corner of the dining room. The caste glass sculpture is illuminated with an uplight at its base. The refraction of the light through the glass is eye-stopping. During the day the piece appears to be a solid dark gray material, like concrete. At night though, the seemingly opaque material comes to life when illuminated. A colored lens can be added to change the whole look of the

In the past, architects and designers have used lighter colors to offset the heat of the desert. Now, as homes are better insulated in the walls and ceilings, and dual-glazed and UV-protected glass doors and windows are more common, it has allowed the palette of finishes to open up. Though lighter finishes create more reflected glare, the richer tones are a lot easier on the eye.

The homeowner did not appreciate mid-century finishes, so out went the blond wood cabinets and in came darker finishes. Whitehead gives much attention to the lighting of kitchens, but it's a particular challenge when the space becomes open to the rest of the house, and the reflective finishes present glare issues. "Now in homes with open plans you can see kitchens from the living room and the dining room, so you want the lighting to flow from area to area," he explains. As with the rest of the house, Whitehead created four levels of lighting— a day-to-day setting, a pass-through setting, an entertaining setting, and a cleanup setting which is the brightest of the four.

A Lutron Grafik Eye dimming system was installed in the main rooms so that with one touch, the mood can change from work mode to a party atmosphere. A Lutron Radio RA system was set up to interface with the Grafik-Eye controls to create a modestly-priced, smart house system. The RA system interfaces with the hardwired dimming controls through a radio frequency. It's a wireless way of providing global controls in a house without opening up walls and ceilings. It's an ideal product to use in existing homes, says Whitehead.

Outside, the desert presents another lighting challenge. Unless a homeowner works with a landscape and lighting designer, the fact that plants grow and cover up lighting fixtures is an often ignored fact which later could turn into a problem. "We worked closely with the landscape designer and contractor. We needed to know what plants they were using, and how big they would get," says Whitehead. "If you water plants daily in the desert, everything grows at a rate five times faster than anywhere else." With that in mind, Whitehead provided an extra length of 5 feet (1.5 m) between the low voltage fixtures he specified. As the plants grow larger, the fixtures can be pulled back to accommodate the growth.

THE ICE BOX

by Güs Wustemann

Swiss architect Gus Wüstemann realizes that most people have a rigid understanding of space and light. "There are four walls, and that's it," he says. "Light becomes just another added item to the room." Wüstemann believes that lighting should be an integrated part of the atmosphere, not just a portion of the design of a home. "When you place a lamp in the middle of a room, you create a clear, defined center and the rest of the space is periphery." Clearly, using a lamp in such a limiting way is a waste of space.

This lighting integration is exactly the philosophy with which he approached the design of this low-budget project that entailed rebuilding a claustrophobic loft space in the attic of a house

in Lucerne, Switzerland. The raw interior work was already finished, so the challenge was to lighten up the rather dark space. However, there were only small roof windows, a skylight, and a terrace on the top floor of the house with an unbeatable view of the town. The terrace was accessible only from a small flight of stairs, and the architectural lines of another floor of the house blocked even more natural light from entering into the attic. The solution was to provide light wherever, and in whatever way, possible. The architect realized he could create a design where the walls were lit from within, as if it were a reflective glacial surface, and then the loft would glow with numerous picks and pockets of light. In addition, Wüstemann took the pressure and constraints off the rectangular loft by using lighting to dissolve each room's borders and turning all the surfaces into a light reflective landscape.

ABOVE: The bathroom in the flat is actually a cube constructed from OSB (oriented strand board)—floor sweepings mixed with glue and formed into board—to replicate that of a large iced-over stone. All of the lighting in the bathroom is indirect fluorescent except at the mirror.

LEFT: The lounge nook is part of the living room when the curtain is open. It's a cubic shape cut from OSB and also frames a light above the built-in couch. The shape, with indirect lighting, is meant to elicit a cavelike environment that might be found hiding in a glacial landscape.

Ice Float

The lighted platform of the bed is crafted to look like a floating piece of ice on a frozen lake. This drifting piece of illuminated "ice" is part of the same landscape story, and even the platform light is dimmable.

Iced-Over Walls

Even the wall behind the platform bed reflects light as if it were bouncing off of a sheet of ice. The effect was achieved by keeping the plaster raw, which was then coated with a two-step, glossy-finish varnish. The result created a surface that replicates the depth of a thickened glacial wall off of which the light bounces from the portable lamps.

Wall Gap

A horizontal lighted gap on the outside bedroom wall signals the entry into the sleeping space. A fluorescent light is integrated within this wall slit so that the indirect light emanates up and out from the gap, and even reflects clearly off of the Puroliss floor.

Called the Glacier, the loft is filled with indirect fluorescent lighting built into the walls and floors throughout the space. This project is a clear example of how important it was for the lighting plan of this loft to be well thought out right at the onset of the construction. The lighting, therefore, became a major integrated part of the loft's design concept and never an afterthought. "All the lighting is quasi-invisible," says Wüstemann. "Light appears to emanate from all the objects that define the space, and it brings all of the objects—and the surfaces—alive." Since the entire loft replicates the feel of a glacier, the built-in furnishings and lights are all part of the spatial concept developed by Wüstemann. The many "blocks of ice" available to sit on, rather than freestanding furniture, also reflect the built-in lighting plan.

Although recessed ceiling fixtures are popular in Europe, Wüstemann chose to forgo that type of lighting in the Glacier's design because the fixtures would be too visible. The same decision was made to eliminate wall and sconce fixtures. Instead, light sources become part of the landscape in the form of crevices that are lit up from within by fluorescent lighting fixtures. Wüstemann crafted the lighting plan so that every light source is dimmable, so the homeowner can create the perfect atmosphere during day or night.

"Even the small, dark cracks in the walls suddenly become interesting if you light up the gap between two materials or objects," says Wüstemann. At night, thin gaps of light, like nature's crevasses created by ice, light up the Glacier and invite all to sit or lie on the landscape and take the time to reflect in its white warmth.

SIMULATING ROCKS

The use of wood on some of the walls in the flat is not only to break up the whiteness, but also as a warm reflective surface for the fluorescent lighting. To create a warm atmosphere to the icy surfaces, Wüstemann used OSB chipboard. "It has a very lively surface, suggesting a rocky surface," explains the architect. "This material is very inexpensive, but in the right context, it looks warm and welcoming."

LIGHTED CURTAIN

The curtain hangs in front of a solid wall, though it appears as if it is drawn over a floor-to-ceiling window. To achieve this lighted look, the architect installed simple fluorescent strip lights along the edge of the floor and on the wall, just behind the curtain. In addition, there is a slit of a skylight above the top of the curtain. In the daytime, natural light streams in from the skylight and hits the back of the fabric. The horizon changes at twilight, when the artificial lighting takes over. As a touch, Wüstemann painted the sides of the skylight gold, so that any light coming in from the outside reflects off the metallic color and takes on the tone of a sunset of an Indian summer evening.

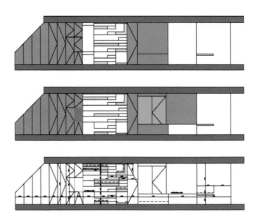

The elevations of the loft show how Wüstemann envisioned the placements of the lighted gaps in the kitchen area.

REFLECTIVE FLOORING

The surface of the floor is a material called Puroliss, produced by Walo Bertschinger, which is a durable polyurethane material used in retail and medical facilities. Its ultra glossy surface reflects the light, yet it is a noise-reducing material.

GLACIAL CABINETRY

Wüstemann used materials and paint to make the flat's landscape look like a glacier of icy edges, especially in the kitchen where all the elements fully disappear behind white cabinets. The cooking surfaces are made from white DuPont Corian, and the cabinets are MDF boards coated in two coats of a white varnish to reflect the indirect fluorescent lighting.

GAPS OF LIGHT

One wall of the kitchen is actually a stairway designed with gaps of light. The indirect fluorescent lights suggest crevices in an iced landscape. It's designed to suggest small-stepped ice blocks. "To make the stairs disappear, I allocated these blocks unevenly," says Wüstemann. "The blocks together with the lighted gaps form a composition. The light gaps are like the leftover voids from where ice blocks emerge on a glacier mountain." All the gaps of light are horizontal except for the L-shaped gap at the top right indicating the direction for the terrace.

BY THE LIGHT OF THE MOON

by Rand Elliott, Elliott + Associates

FLOATING CEILING

The wall adjacent to the master bedroom's closet is 1-foot (30 cm) lower than the other walls in the room. Elliott used cove lighting only on that wall for two reasons. First, he wanted to create a hot line of light above the bed to bring ambient lighting into the room. Second, the line of light gives the eye the perception that the ceiling is floating. The line of light fills in the one-foot (30 cm) -difference, visually pushing up the ceiling. This technique is effective in spaces where the homeowner prefers to hide lighting and keep walls free from fixtures.

RECESSED WALL WASHERS

In addition to the cove lighting, a line of low-voltage recessed wall washers with diffuser lenses are placed above the bed over the pillow area—the optimum placement for overhead reading lights. The fixtures are angled to evenly illuminate the artwork, and the light bounces off the wall and onto the bed area for soft reading light without glare. For uniform illumination, Elliott placed the row of fixtures 3 feet (0.9 m) out from the wall, and they are placed three feet apart from one another. The homeowners had a special request for the recessed fixtures, says Elliott. Half the fixtures over the bed work independently from the other half. That way, if one person wants to read and the other wants to sleep, each can turn on or turn off the lights over their side of the bed. Above the window, Elliott placed more recessed, adjustable fixtures that have a slotted aperture, giving off a narrow beam so that the light does not hit the windows and create glare or reflection.

The lighting plan of this modern glass house subtly highlights the craggy natural landscape surrounding the Oklahoma home as much as it brings elements of it indoors. The homeowner was able to convince the developer to allow the construction of a contemporary house in a neighborhood full of traditional architecture. One of the conditions was that the house had to be nearly invisible from the street, during the daytime and the nighttime—an issue that the correct lighting plan would help to handle. Architect Rand Elliott set forth on the mandates by removing as few existing trees as possible on the site, and by placing the glass house on a natural land ridge that would bring in more natural light during the day.

The goal, to blend the architecture together with the soil the house sits on, is guided by the lighting design that is woven throughout the interior. The lighting plan creates a serene, quiet light throughout the house that brings in reminders of the outside—for example, a lighted lavender-colored panel gives visitors a hint of the purple haze seen on the horizon.

The lighting design starts at the exterior entryway's pathway lighting. In keeping with the developer's request that the house blend in seamlessly with the landscape, Elliott let nature take the lead right at the front door. "There is no ambient lighting on the walkway except for the romantic glow of the moon," says Elliott.

During the nighttime, the interior of the home seems to "pop" when viewed from the outside. It's an intentional design because the house is mostly all glass. If the lighting is not done properly, there would be too many reflections of the interior seen on the windows during the nighttime, and those sorts of reflections can confuse the eye and block uninterrupted views to the outside. The lighting is the main factor that allows the dominant artwork in the house—which is the natural landscape, along with dramatic weather conditions—to be highlighted and clearly viewed through the large expanses of glass.

Dark Flooring

White walls let the art stand out from the walls, and the richly colored, dark flooring is concrete-stained in a color that matches the rich, earthy color of the soil outside. It is like walking on dirt, in the most sensual way. By having a dark floor and light ceilings and walls, the floor is diffusing and creates a warm "fill light" effect.

Skylight

Just 6 feet (1.8 meters) inside the entryway is a pivotal lighting fixture that illuminates an outdoor art niche. The circular skylight is 2 feet (0.6 meter) in diameter and lights the sculpture all day with daylight. At night, the skylight has a low voltage of artificial light in an aluminum housing with an outdoor ballast to withstand the cold Oklahoma weather. The dual-purpose skylight is an important architectural element because it can be seen from the entryway, the living room, and the master bedroom.

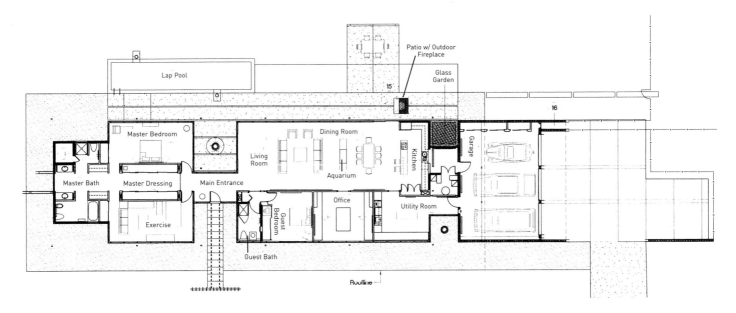

Master Bath

Master Dressing

Master Bedroom

Lap Pool

Exercise

Main Entrance

Guest Bedroom

Guest Bath

Living Room

Dining Room

Aquarium

Office

Kitchen

Utility Room

Patio w/ Outdoor Fireplace

Glass Garden

15'

16

Garage

Roofline

The house lays long and low in the landscape, so that each room benefits from the
expanses of glass windows that bring in a
vast amount of daylight. Only the master
dressing room is centered within the core
of the interior. To supplement natural light,
Elliott designed a clean, simple lighting
plan that relies on strategically placed
recessed fixtures.

Though the interior pops, Elliott designed the
level of brightness indoors to stay low. To
achieve that sort of light-and-dark contrast with
low levels of light, Elliott focused on using
downlights, wall washers, and spotlights
instead of using fixtures that would produce
larger pools of ambient light. Because of the
low-level interior lighting plan, the objects outside the house have a slight glow around them.
The low-level exterior lighting plan creates
another magical occurrence at night. When all
the indoor lights are shut off, all reflections on
the windows disappear and the glass windows
become virtually invisible to the eye. When that
happens, the homeowners feel as though they
are outside.

One of the lighting plan's surprises is the 500-
gallon (1,893 l) -aquarium that divides the living
and dining space. The light that shimmers within the freestanding saltwater aquarium provides
a serene sense of movement between the
rooms. The homeowners find the ambiance so
magical that they dine there all the time bask-
ing solely in the aquarium light. When only
these lights are on, it creates a reflection of the
tank, and the feeling is that of sitting within a
glowing waterscape. Elliott achieved the dramatic effects by lighting the tank from above
rather than from within the confines of the
tank. "By illuminating the aquarium from above
the water, the light bounces off of the water
and up to the ceiling, says Elliott. "It creates a
much more atmospheric dining experience."

ABOVE: Moonlight is the major source of nighttime illumination for the front walkway. However, concealed lighting underneath the steel entry-bridge brightens the gravel for safety reasons even though the lighted slits are actually gaps between the steel panels. Linear fluorescent bulbs that are affixed under the edge of the panels create the illumination that shines upward from the gaps.

OPPOSITE ABOVE: The typical way to light an aquarium is to place special fluorescent bulbs in the tank or under the cover of the tank. Instead of fluorescent fixtures, Elliott installed low-voltage, recessed lighting in the ceiling above the tank to achieve two effects. First, narrow spots (each with a tiny 7-degree aperture) with 50-watt MR-16 bulbs create columns of light that stream down into the water (the cover is left off the aquarium to let more moisture into the air and to reflect light). The effect is like that of rays of sunlight piercing the water's surface and sent streaming down to the bottom. The second effect created is that of a shimmering shadow of water reflected onto the ceiling.

OPPOSITE BELOW: Above the kitchen counter is a glowing, lighted opening that acts as art. The violet illumination in the kitchen was crafted using a sheet rock wall with a square hole cut in it, a 6-inch (15 cm) space backed by another wall. To create the horizon-like feature, there is a T8 color-corrected fluorescent lamp with a blue gel placed between the two walls. The gradation of the purple light gives the kitchen a mysterious quality. Elliott chose a color-corrected lamp to keep the color temperature the same throughout the house. "The one thing I don't like is walking into a house and seeing different color temperatures from room to room because of the bulbs being used," says Elliott. "Maybe one room feels warm in color temperature, another feels too blue in color temperature. Keeping a consistent color temperature throughout the house is a lighting design detail that is often overlooked by homeowners."

SHEETS OF LIGHT

by Akihito Fumita, Fumita Design Office

The staircase connects each of the floors both physically and visually with light, says Fumita. The way the staircase is illuminated is also a safety factor for the garage during the nighttime.

This brilliantly lighted house made quite a splash in this quiet residential street in suburban Tokyo. The client, who is in the construction business, frequently worked with architect Akihito Fumita, and knew of his glass, metal, and all-white designs. The house—for himself, his wife, and two young children—would also be designed—and illuminated—to highlight his cars. "One of his requests was that he wanted the house *not* to look like a house, and that he wanted the house to stand out and be something that people would marvel at," says Fumita. "Another request was that the house would be arranged so he could see his two cars from within the house."

Fumita, who prefers to install indirect lighting for both residential design and retail and public space design, used the technique throughout this home. The architect is a strong believer that light fixtures should provide illumination, but never be seen. "Indirect lighting secures the practical brightness needed in a home, and it can define the special volume and elements of a space," says Fumita. "However, if this technique is used only for the sake of using a popular technique, and it is not well integrated into a home's design, it tends to end up having a boring or disastrous appearance." To eliminate any visual clutter that lighting may have provided, Fumita built all fixtures into the walls and covered the lamps with white acrylic panels.

ROOFTOP

The staircase was designed to be a light well, letting the natural light penetrate in from the rooftop down to the garage. The natural light bounces and reflects into all three stories of the home.

CURVED LIGHTS

During the night, the edge of the staircase's opening lights up. These curved lights reflect onto the glass treads to create a shimmering tube of light.

TREADS

The treads of the spiral staircase are crafted from nonslip glass so that the light passes through each stair and up into the living room.

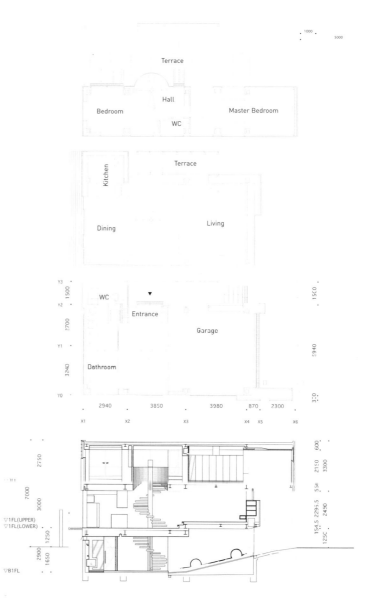

ABOVE: The kitchen is the place of work, says Fumita, so he designed the lighting in a basic workable style that would not hinder tasks in the space.

OPPOSITE PAGE, ABOVE: The client's cars were very important, and he wanted to be able to see them while relaxing in his house. To achieve this, Fumita designed the garage so that the client would exit his car and walk through a glass wall where the entrance hall and the spiral staircase were placed. Across the entry hall is the bathroom, so that he can view the cars from the tub, as well. "The expanded metal floor of the garage is lit up from underneath, as if it's a stage for the car or as if it's a display in a showroom," says Fumita.

OPPOSITE PAGE, BELOW: The bathroom is located in the home's basement level for a clear view to the client's cars. The bathroom has four downlights for ambient lighting. Slim fluorescent lamps are placed behind the long mirror and the wooden cylinders, which are the storage cupboards. The damp location limited the architect's preferred and complicated indirect lighting technique, but Fumita was able to hide much of the lighting equipment.

In Japan, there are restrictions that do not allow any new house to be built that would cast a shadow on surrounding residential structures for more than a few hours daily. Fumita took advantage of this flow of unobstructed natural light by giving the three-level house a functional light tube, or a circular staircase, that even funnels light down into the garage area as shown in the floor plans and elevation.

This house is neither boring nor disastrous. It is, however, a study of how light has been integrated into the materials of the house. "I regard light as one of a number of elements that compose a space, like a wall or a floor, and as a material like glass or metal," says Fumita. Because his client requested an all-white home, Fumita designed all-white objects, with built-in sources of white light, to help express each space of the house. "By working in white, I could concentrate in thinking about the form and the light without the noise of color," he says. "I don't dislike using color, but my interest is more in the manipulation of form and light, and that worked well for this home."

The centerpiece of the house is its circular staircase that spans three levels and is topped by a circular skylight. It acts like a tube that lets in natural light, but he integrated artificial lighting into the structure, as well. Fumita used mostly fluorescent lighting in the house, and sprinkled in some dichloic halogen lamps in table lamps and recessed ceiling spots in a few key areas. "By concealing fluorescent lights, I like the way the light pools in between the gaps where physical volumes meet," he says. "This way, it looks as if sheets of light appear to emerge between where the two planes meet."

ABOVE: Another view of the living room shows how the all-white interior is a study in restraint, chosen to reduce visual clutter. Walls, cabinets, and doors in the living room recede, making the small floor appear larger. However, reflective white paint helps natural and artificial light bounce off surfaces for a brighter effect.

BELOW: The perfectly symmetrical bedroom is rather small, and there is only enough room to place a bed. The bed and headboard were custom-designed to fit the room. Concealing slim, seamless fluorescent tubular lights with an acrylic cover illuminates the headboard. Fumita customdesigned the table lamps as a gift for his client. The light from the table lamps reflects off of aluminum blinds on the highset square windows flanking the bed. All the lights in the bedroom are dimmable.

SPOTS

Two discreet spotlights are aimed onto corner alcoves that are used for objects. The light gives off just enough illumination to brighten up the corners of the beds, so it's easier and safer to walk around the piece of furniture without stubbing toes.

CLOSET DOORS

Fluorescent tubes were built into the tops of the closet doors and then covered with acrylic.

WINDOWS

At the other end is the entry door to the bedroom, then a passageway with two closet walls. Fluorescent tube lights were used to brighten the narrow space and were hidden up along the ribbon windows above the doorway.

CEILING

"The ceiling levels are pretty complicated here because of the need for structural beams," says Fumita. "To disguise the messy situation, I lit up the ceiling surface so that it looks lighter than it really is." He concealed fluorescent lights so that the tubes would not be spotted.

A HOME BRIMMING WITH HEIRLOOM LIGHTS

by Mark Brazier-Jones Studio

"Designers never provide strong enough hooks in the ceiling for chandeliers," says Brazier-Jones. "A decent fixing should be able to hold a man swinging from it!" Brazier-Jones prefers to place a chandelier, such as his Sera Pendant Light, over a bed for a subtle glow.

OPPOSITE PAGE: Brazier-Jones set up a glowing vignette of light in his living room to include many of his lighting designs, including Diamond Candleholders. A string of twinkling pink lights is carefully wrapped around a statue of a Madonna and child. The designer's Shakti Mirror, a cast resin and beveled glass with a gold leaf frame, reflects the light into the living room.

Mark Brazier-Jones is an influential and internationally known name in lighting design, and he happily bucks the trends of the field. His philosophies are quite evident when a reveal of his own home is shown. "In my opinion, there are a number of sins when it comes to lighting design today," he says. "For one, I detest using 12V downlights above a bed, a bathtub, or over a sofa—the high-pitched glare of the fixtures in the eyes at night goes against nature's intention of living with the warm glow of a fire." Another sin, Brazier-Jones says, is the overuse of lighting system panels on every wall. "It takes a nuclear scientist to know how to use the settings," he says. "There are miles and miles of wires and cables used for these situations, and one day something will go wrong and we will all have to go back to the basics."

It is the basic mode of lighting—from candles to simple incandescent bulbs—that makes Brazier-Jones happy, especially when it comes to his own home and accompanying studio, which are both located in a sixteenth-century barn just outside of London. Though his home is his retreat, Brazier-Jones also uses it as an R&D lab, experimenting with materials and creating prototypes—mostly in metal and glass— for his well-known clients.

Brazier-Jones is known for creating fixtures with an heirloom quality to them. "My pieces are made robustly," he says. "They will last for centuries. The technology I use is simple and will always exist so any parts will be easily replaced."

To create a fixture, Brazier-Jones takes a piece of metal and a bulb, then moves a glass lens around it to see how the light bounces off of walls. "I don't sit in front of a CAD machine to create fixtures, and it's not my intention to know how light-efficient my light fixtures are," he says. Brazier-Jones's intention is to get the world back to the simplicity of lighting, the sparkle of light coming off a crystal glass droplet, or a glistening chandelier twinkling over the dining room table. "My favorite light source, after all, is a clear (not frosted) 60-watt candle bulb on a dimmer. It's simple, and it does the job well to create an enhancing and controlled glow in a home."

Candles are also frequent lighting sources in Brazier-Jones's house. "I don't like a bright house, and my home is really designed for nighttime use," says Brazier-Jones. "Most lighting designers are interested in creating as much light as possible with a fixture, but I'm interested in the opposite; I'm interested in creating shadows."

Brazier-Jones calls it the "dappled light effect" that he tries to recreate all the time through his fixtures. By placing numerous fixtures that are encased or studded with glass balls and lenses, and often detailed with filigree metalwork, he

RIGHT: One of Brazier-Jones's favorite lighting sources is a wall sconce, such as the Olympia fixture he designed and installed in his bathroom. The metal fixture has a glass lens that magnifies the candle-like light of the bulb. The fixture can be converted to accept electric bulbs, as well. Heat-treated copper leaves surround the lens, and colored glass balls reflect light like a prism.

OPPOSITE PAGE: The entryway of Brazier-Jones's home encapsulates his lighting philosophy. He uses candles to create a welcoming glow, and in the corner, he hung a Sera Wall Lantern. The blue glow comes from one of the designer's earlier light fixtures, called Auralight, which is no longer in production. The Sera Lantern has lenses and glass balls that are laced with filigree metalwork to create that dappled light effect that Brazier-Jones is fond of. The puddles of light and leafy shadows are cast about the room by both electric and candlelight (with drip trays).

has succeeded in creating puddles of light and shadow throughout his home—from the entryway to the bathroom.

But what is most important to Brazier-Jones is the fact that he is creating lighting with staying power that can be used in any interior whether it is traditional or contemporary. His home and his designs, though eclectic upon first sight, incorporate classic materials—such as metal and glass—in timeless ways. "I am impressed by things that are built to last," he says. "An engine that still does its work after one hundred years—that excites me. Something that is so good you never want to replace it. That is something worthy of respect." And that is the uncomplicated philosophy by which Brazier-Jones designs his lighting fixtures.

RIGHT: A living room is the most difficult space to light, says Brazier-Jones. "It's multifunctional and there needs to be a few different options for mood lighting," he says. Two to three different circuits, each on a simple dimmer, would control the table lights, wall sconces, and overhead lighting. Here, Brazier-Jones' glass floor lamps (including a bulb aiming up onto a silver ball) augment the central lighting source of the fireplace.

BELOW: The Dew Lamp, designed by Brazier-Jones looks like two illuminated raindrops on a pedestal. The black iron fixture stands on three bronze legs. The forged steel and glass filigree shade and bronze finial envelope a 60-watt bulb.

GLOSSARY OF LIGHTING TERMS

A-lamp/A-type lamp: The standard common household incandescent light bulb.

Accent lighting: A light used to accentuate an object or architectural element.

ADA fixtures: Wall fixtures extending less than 4 inches from the wall to comply with the Americans with Disabilities Act.

Ambient light: General source of light that uniformly illuminates entire room, typically from a ceiling fixture or near-ceiling suspended fixture that delivers large pool of light in space.

Alternating Current (AC): Electric current that reverses direction at regular intervals. Standard AC in US is 60 hertz per second; standard AC in Europe is 50 hertz per second.

Amperes/amps: The unit of measurement of electrical current.

Aperture: The opening of a fixture through which light shines.

Architectural lighting: Term for built-in, hard-wired, or direct-wired lighting fixtures.

Argon: Gas used inside most incandescent light bulbs.

Baffle: Part of a fixture (plates, grooves, other accessories) used to block light preventing glare and controls brightness, often painted black to absorb light.

Ballast: Electrical device that provides current to start up fluorescent lamps and bulbs.

Base: Bottom part of table or floor lamp on which a shade sits; also part of light bulb that is inserted into socket—screw-in for incandescent or pin designs for CFL.

Beam spread: Measurement of the angle (narrow, wide) of a light beam from a lamp with a reflector.

BIAX lamp: Also known as a Compact Fluorescent Lamp (CFL).

Can: Also known as housing for recessed downlights.

Candela: A unit of measurement of the luminous intensity coming from a light source.

Candle-foot or foot-candle: Unit for measuring illumination, equal to the amount of direct light thrown off by one candle on a square foot (0.3 sq m) of surface. Also known as "lux" in Europe.

Canopy: Fixture part that covers an outlet/electrical junction box.

Compact Fluorescent Lamp (CFL): Energy efficient bulb. It uses 67 percent less energy than a standard incandescent bulb. A standard 75-watt bulb is comparable to a 20-watt CFL in light output. It's also available for outdoor use. Also known as BIAX lamps.

Color filter: Accessory placed over lamps to create colored light beams.

CRI (Color Rendering Index): The closer CRI of a lamp is to 100, the more "true" it renders color in the room. Full spectrum lamps offer CRIs of over 90. A bulb with a CRI in the 80s offers good color rendering, as well. Multiple phosphor coatings on a bulb can increase the CRI of a lamp so that objects under the light source show truer colors. For example, most fluorescent lamps have a CRI of between 70 and 80+.

Cross lighting: A technique used when spot or floodlights are mounted to both sides of a tree, gate, or arbor to softly highlight details and shadows.

Current: Flow of electricity measured in amps.

Damp rating: Many building codes require that a fixture have a UL Damp Rating when used outdoors in a damp location. However, damp-rated fixtures cannot be used in areas exposed directly to precipitation.

Diffused lighting: Light from one source that appears to be dispersed, creating a softened effect.

Diffuser: Device in any number of materials that covers or shades a bulb and creates the effect of diffused light.

Dimmer: Control that varies output of light source by reducing voltage or current to a lamp. Dimmers enhance atmosphere and reduce the amount of power used to extend the life of incandescent light bulbs. (Please note that compact fluorescent light bulbs typically cannot be dimmed.)

Direct lighting: A form of illumination where 90 percent or more of the light is cast downward.

Downlighting: Effect of recessed lights in a ceiling.

Efficacy: A way to tell the efficiency of a light bulb; the higher the lumens per watt (LPW), the more light emitted.

Extended Life Lamp: Incandescent lamp with 2,500+ hours of rated average life and reduced output with stronger filament.

Eyeball: A recessed, adjustable accent light protruding slightly below ceiling.

Filament: Wire coil made of tungsten that produces light when heated by an electric current.

Fill gas: Gas in a light bulb, such as argon or krypton for incandescent bulbs, halogen in halogen bulbs.

Fluorescent bulb: Belongs to the group of lighting devices known collectively as discharge tubes—glass tubes filled with metal vapor with electrodes at both tube ends. Electric current that is passed between the electrodes eventually ionizes the vapor, which begins to glow, producing light. Fluorescent lamps emit more light per watt than incandescent bulbs, last ten times longer. Their light is generally whiter and cooler than incandescent bulbs. If the chemicals in the interior phosphor coating are changed, different light tones—such as the light that mimics sunlight, can be produced. Fluorescents are limited in exterior use because although ballasts start the lamps in cold weather, the lamps themselves operate better in interior temperatures. In addition, extreme temperatures affect the performance of the lamp. Regular fluorescent lighting requires a special ballast for dimming.

Flight paper: Decorative heat-resistant paper used as shading for bulbs.

Floodlighting: A very wide light beam from a reflector bulb.

Foot-candle or candle foot: Common measurement of light levels, the amount of illumination on a surface one foot away from a common candle. For many years these lighting calculations for interiors were made to provide uniform illumination on working surfaces; i.e. one foot-candle is one lumen on a square-foot of a surface.

Framing projector: A spotlight with attachments allowing accurate control over the shape and focus of the beam—useful for accenting artwork or photography.

Frosted glass: Lightbulbs treated with spray coating for opacity.

Full spectrum lighting: Bulbs designed to accurately mimic natural sunlight.

G-lamp: Globe-shaped lightbulbs

Gimbal lighting: Adjustable ring that holds a PAR or MR lamp in place.

Globe: Round bulb used without shade in a bath fixture.

Grazing: Painting a wall, surface, or feature with light.

Halogen lamp: Sometimes shown as "halogena" —a bulb that contains halogen gases meant to extend life of a tungsten filament through a recycling system known as a halogen cycle. The bulbs are hotter than A-type and produce more LPW (lumens per watt) of bright, pure white light. It costs more to purchase, but is more efficient. It lasts 3 times longer, produces 50 percent more light for the same amount of energy used.

Hard back: Lamp shade lined with plastic.

Harp: Device used to attach a shade onto a lamp.

Hertz: Cycles per second for alternating currents.

Housing: Also known as cans for track lighting fixtures.

IC-type fixture or Insulated Ceiling Fixture: A recessed downlighting fixture suitable for direct placement in a ceiling's thermal insulation.

IF: Inside frosted bulb.

Incandescent bulb: Standard type also called A-type bulb (most popular for its warm, flattering color). Category is comprised of any bulb with a filament, including standard tungsten, halogen, and xenon bulb. The filament is heated to a point of glowing. The glowing filament produces the bulb's stable, bright, and long-lasting light.

Kilowatt hour: A one-hour unit of measurement of electrical energy. One kilowatt hour equals 1000 watts energy.

Lamp: Professional term for lightbulb.

Light source: A fixture, lamp, or natural light that illuminates a space.

Light trespass: When a fixture's light beam goes past the property and into a neighbor's yard for creating unwanted illumination.

Line-volt: 120 volt for US standards; 220 volt for European standards.

Louvers: A screen of multiple baffles on a fixture that is meant to diffuse light.

Low-voltage: Lamps with 6 or 12 volts that require a transformer connected to a standard voltage power source.

Lumens: Standard measure of light produced by a bulb. A standard 100-watt bulb produces about 1600 lumens. Technically called "luminous flux."

Luminaire: A light fixture.

Lux: The international standard unit for measuring light levels (as opposed to foot-candles in the U.S.); one lumen per square meter.

Mogul base: Lamp base for high-wattage bulbs.

Moonlighting: Also known as "downlighting" in a landscape. Replicates natural moonlight by shining light down from tree or high post. The soft light casts shadows.

MR lamp: Multifaceted reflector lamp. MR-16 is the most popular type. MR lamps surrounded by halogen capsule with a computer-designed glass or metal reflector with many facets. These lenses require a glass cover.

Parabolic Aluminized Reflector (PAR): Outdoor flood bulb resistant to damp areas used for spotlighting or as flood lights. An extremely bright light providing 4 times the light of regular incandescent bulbs. Used in recessed and track lighting. Weatherproof casing makes it suitable for outdoor use. Also available in halogen.

Pendant fixtures: Suspended light fixture.

Photometrics: The measurement of the intensity of light from a fixture or lamp.

Pinhole: Recessed downlight with a faceplate with small aperture used for narrow beams of light.

Portable fixture: Lighting fixture that includes cord and plug.

Post-top fixture: Outdoor fixture that marks property entrance.

Power pack (low voltage): Also called a transformer. It supplies electricity for 100 watts and plugs into a standard outlet, reducing regular household current (120V) to a safe 12V.

Pendant fixtures: Drops the light source away from the ceiling and down into a space, good for task lighting, bringing the light source closer to the work area without overlighting the rest of the room.

Puck light: A generic term for shallow halogen under-cabinet fixture that looks like a hockey puck.

Quartz halogen: A quartz glass which withstands high pressure of halogen lamp, but transmits more UV radiation than ordinary glass.

Recessed downlights: Cans, or housing, for lamps that are mounted into a ceiling.

Reflected glare: Also known as veiling reflections. This is the glare that results from light shining off of polished or glossy surfaces.

Reflector: Device used in a fixture to reflect light in a chosen direction or desired brightness, used in a spot or recessed fixture.

Scene: Pre-set settings on dimmers.

Sconce: Wall-mounted fixture.

Shielding: Umbrella term for diffusers, baffles, louvers, shades.

Specular: Mirror finish on a fixture's surface.

Spot light: Narrow beam of light.

Starter: *See* Ballast.

Swing-arm fixture: Adjustable horizontal arm used to position a wall or table lamp.

Surface-mounted fixture: A ceiling-mounted fixture.

Suspended fixture: Also known as pendant and hangs from ceiling.

Switch leg: Name of the wire between light fixture and dimmer switch.

Task lighting: Focused beam of light for reading, cooking, grooming, workshop activities, sewing, typically in form of desk lamp, table/floor lamp, low-hanging pendants.

Three-way lamp: Incandescent bulb with filaments designed for three levels of light. Small filament is used for low light level, larger filament for medium light and both filaments turn on together to create high level of light.

Toggle: Common control switch on lamps.

Torchiere: Floor light with bowl diffuser sending indirect light up to ceiling.

Transformer: See power pack.

Trim: Decorative accessory covering rough opening to a recessed lighting fixture can.

UL damp rating: *See* damp rating.

UL rating: A rigorous safety test given to electrical products by the Underwriter's Laboratory.

Uplighting: Technique of illuminating from the underside of an object or plant. It is the opposite of natural daylight—creates a soft glow highlighting sculptural quality of trees, bushes, or objects.

Valance lighting: Architectural fixtures installed behind horizontal shield along perimeter of room or above one or more windows.

Vanity lighting: Fixtures above or beside a bathroom mirror.

Vapor tight luminaire: Fixture resistant to water vapor created by steam in kitchens and baths.

Veiling reflections: *See* reflected glare.

Volt: Unit of electrical force or pressure. In US, 120 volts average. In Europe, 240 volts average.

Wall grazing: Technique to create dramatic shadows on surfaces.

Wall lighting: Light that bounces off wall to give appearance of spaciousness.

Wallwashing: Technique bathes wall in light to emphasize space, fixtures direct beams of light at wall. This technique gives impression the space is expanded, gives feeling of more space in a room. Wallwashers can be recessed or surface-mounted on tracks.

Wand fixture: Type of track lighting fixture that precisely directs light beam.

Watt: A unit of electrical power.

Wattage: The amount of electricity consumed by a bulb to produce light.

Well lights: Inground landscape fixture that throws light up and out to highlight an object or a wall.

Xenon bulb: New type of incandescent bulb, cooler and longer-lasting than halogens, but still runs warmer and less efficient than fluorescent.

Zone lighting: Selection of fixtures operated by one dimmer or control. There can be more than one zone in one room. In addition, the lighting of one or more rooms can be ganged together and turned on remotely by a zone-controlling device.

CONTRIBUTING LIGHTING DESIGNERS, ARCHITECTS, AND INTERIOR DESIGNERS

ADOLFO PEREZ ARCHITECT
69 Union Street
Newton, MA 02459 USA
T: 617-527-7442
F: 617-527-3757
W: www.adolfoperez.com
E: office@adolfoperez.com
Project: Illuminating a Retreat
[Page 84]

AJS DESIGN
Abigail Shachat
325 West 38th Street #412
New York, NY 10018 USA
T: 212-643-8043
F: 212-643-9654
W: www.ajsdesignsnyc.com
E: info@ajsdesignsnyc.com
Project. Stretching Space With Light
[Page 134]

AVALON ARTISTIC LANDSCAPE
LIGHTING
Mark Carlson
8150 Greenback Lane, #200
Fair Oaks, CA 95628 USA
T. 916-780-2205
C: 916-532-9699
W: www.avalonlighting.com
Projects:
A Play of Light and Shadows
[Page 122]
Techniques of the Trade
[Page 128]

CATALANO ARCHITECTS
Tom Catalano
115 Broad Street
Boston, MA 02110 USA
T: 617-338-7447
F: 617-338-6639
W: www.catalanoinc.com
[Page 102]

CHAPMAN ARCHITECTS
Meg Chapman
185 Varick Street
New York, NY 10014 USA
T: 212-620-0972
W: www.chapmanarchitects.com
E: meg@chapmanarchitects.com
Project: A Chef's Delight—builder of
kitchen, Pier Head Associates, LTD.
[Page 90]

C&D DESIGN
Connie Driscoll
W: www.CND-Design.com
E: connie@CND-Design.com
Project: A Layering of Loveliness
[Page 64]

D-SQUARED
Mark Hewitt
1 Hatfield House
Baltic Street West
London EC14 0ST UK
T: 44 (0) 20-7253-2240
W: www.d2-design.co.uk
E: mark@d2-design.co.uk
Project: Capturing Daylight
[Page 86]

DAVID LING ARCHITECT
225 East 21st Street
New York, NY 10010 USA
T: 212-982-7089
F: 212-475-1336
W: www.davidlingarchitect.com
E:lingarchitect@verizon.net
Projects:
The Shelf Life of Light
[Page 56]
A Crisp White Light
[Page 78]

DESIGNWORKER
Ed Grogan
T: 413-587-9476
C: 413-538-0952
W: www.designworkder.net
E: ed@designworker.net
Project: Night Light
[Page 106]

DESIGN GALLERIA
T: 404-261-3208
Project: [Page 89]

DMAC ARCHITECTURE
Dwayne MacEwen
1418 N. Kingsbury Street
Chicago, IL 60622 USA
T: 312-573-1237
F: 312-573-1236
W: www.dmacarch.com
E: dmacewen@dmacarch.com
Projects.
The Pampered Kitchen and Bath
[Page 98]
Walls of Light
[Page 107]

DUFFY DESIGN
Dennis Duffy
1313 Washington Street, Suite 505
Boston, MA 02118 USA
T: 617-542-2074
F: 617-542-2075
W: www.duffydesigngroup.com
E: Info@duffydesigngroup.com
Project: A Designer's Own Lighting
Plan
[Page 94]

ELLIOTT & ASSOCIATES
Rand Elliott, FAIA
Elliott + Associates
35 Harrison Avenue
Oklahoma City, OK 73104 USA
T: 405-232-9554
F: 405-232-9997
W: www.e-a-a.com
Projects: [Page 36],
Boxed Brilliance
[Page 72]
By the Light of the Moon
[Page 150]

ERICKSON ZEBROSKI DESIGN GROUP
Chet Zebroski, Laurie Erickson
1246 18th Street, San Francisco, CA
94107 USA
T: 415-487-8660
W: www.ezdg.net
E: mail@ezdg.net
Project: A Radiant Redwood Bath
[Page 92]

FRANK ROOP DESIGN & INTERIORS
129 Newbury Street
Suite 201
Boston, MA 02116 USA
T: 617-267-0818
F: 617-267-3342
W: www.frankroop.com
E: frank@frankroop.com
Project: Couture Lighting
[Page 50]

FUMITA DESIGN OFFICE
T:+81-3-5414-2880
F:+81-3-5414-2881
W: www.fumitadesign.com
E: mail@fumitadesign.com
Project: Sheets of Light
[Page 156]

GLEYSTEEN DESIGN
Marcus Gleysteen
185 Mt. Auburn Street
Cambridge, MA 02138 USA
T: 617-492-6060
W: www.gleysteen design.com
Project: [Page 8]

GUS WÜSTEMANN
Köchlistrasse 15
T: +4112956016
C: +41796347340
F: +4112956019
W: www.guswutemann.com
E: architects@guswutemann.com
Projects:
The New Fireplace
[Page 54]
The Ice Box
[Page 146]
An Optical Illusion
[Page 112]

IGLOO DESIGN GROUP, INC.
Tracey Sawyer
185 Varick Street, Suite 505
New York, NY 10014 USA
T: 212-620-0972
C: 917-443-1906
F: 212-504-9527
W: www.igloodesigngroup.com
E: tracey.sawyer@igloodesigngroup.com
Project: A Canopy of Lighted Coves
[Page 46]

INTERIOR CONSTRUCTION SERVICES
T: 303-442-4166
Project: Vignettes of Light
(Page 60)

JAN MOYER DESIGN
T: 518-235-4756
W: www.janmoyer.com
E: moyerj@nycap.rr.com
Projects: (Page 13),
An Outdoor Destination
(Page 114)
The Light Down the Hal
(Page 105)

JONATHAN HOPP INTERIOR DESIGN
11271 Ventura Blvd.
Studio City, CA 91604 USA
T: 818-472-6001
F: 818-763-4739
W: www.jonathanhopp.com
E: jonhopp@pacbell.net
Project: A House with a Light Touch
(Page 140)

KANNER ARCHITECTS
10924 Le Conte Avenue
Los Angeles, CA 90024 USA
T: 310-208-0028
F: 310-208-5756
W: www.kannerarch.com
E: info@kannerarch.com
Project: A Subtle Beacon of Light
(Page 126, 132)

KAR-HWA HO ARCHITECT
117 West 17th Street, Suite 4C
New York, NY 10011 USA
T: 212 989-2693
F: 212 647-1894
E: khoarchitect@aol.com
Projects:
Planes of Light
(Page 58)
Mood Lighting
(Page 76)

LEDBETTER FULLERTON ARCHITECTS
Lee H. Ledbetter
1055 St. Charles Av, Suite 320
New Orleans, LA 70130 USA
T: 504-566-9669
F: 504-566-9668
W: www.Lfarchitects.com
Projects:
The Art of Light
(Page 40)
Light Dock
(Page 80)

MARK BRAZIER-JONES STUDIO
Lighting Designer
Hyde Hall Barn Sandon
Buntingford. Hertfordshire SG9 ORU
T: 0044(0)1763 273 599
F: 0044(0)1763 273 410
W: www.brazier-jones.com
E: studio@brazier-jones.com
Project: A Home Brimming With
Heirloom Lights
(Page 162)

MARK KUBICKI LIGHTING DESIGN
Mark J. Kubicki
57 Montague Street
Brooklyn, NY 11201 USA
E: Mark.Kubicki@verizon.net
Projects:
Planes of Light
(Page 58)
Mood Lighting
(Page 76)

MICHAEL GLASSMAN & ASSOCIATES
5623 H Street
Sacramento, CA 95819 USA
T: 916-736-2222
W: www.michaelglassman.com
Project: A Play of Light & Shadows
(Page 122)

RANDALL WHITEHEAD LIGHTING, INC.
1246 18th Street, San Francisco, CA
94107 USA
T: 415-626-1277
W: www.randallwhitehead.com
E: rdw@randallwhitehead.com
Projects: (Page 110)
Renewing a Kitchen With Light
(Page 96)
A Radiant Redwood Bath
(Page 92)
A House With a Light Touch
(Page 140)

RENEE PRICE DESIGN
846 Charles Allen Drive
Atlanta, GA 30308 USA
T: 917-825-0749
E: price.renee@gmail.com
Project: A Canopy of Lighted Coves
(Page 46)

RON YEO ARCHITECT, INC.
500 Jasmine Avenue
Corona Del Mar, CA 92625 USA
T: 949-644-8111
F: 949-644-0449
W: www.ronyeo.com
E: ron@ronyeo.com
Project: The Flow of Light
(Page 120)

SAIA BARBARESE TOPOUZANOV
ARCHITECTS
339, Rue St-Paul Est, 3e Étage
Montréal, Québec H2Y 1H3 Canada
T: 514-866-2085
F: 514-874-0233
W: www.sbt.qc.ca
E: sbt@sbt.qc.ca
Project: The Wonder of Nature's Light
(Page 68)

SIMON CONDER ASSOCIATES
Architects + Designers
Nile Street Studios
8 Nile Street
London N1 7RF
UK
T: 44 (0) 20-7251-2144
F: 44 (0) 20-7251-2145
W: www.simonconder.co.uk
E: sca@simonconder.co.uk
Project: Underlighting a Living Space
(Page 66)

SIMON DAVIES, LIGHTING DESIGNER
London West 8 AB Gallery
Odengatan 26
113 51
Stockholm, Sweden
T: + 46 8 673 7330
F: + 46 8 673 7335
W: www.londonw8.se
Project: Lighting a Rich, Dark Space
(Page 108)

VERBECK DESIGN STUDIOS INC.
Laurence Verbeck, Architect, A.I.A.
P.O. Box 1663
Boulder, CO 80306 USA
T: 303-926-6909
C: 303-931-9386
F: 303-926-6720
W: www.Verbeckdesign.com
E: Renzo@Verbeckdesign.com
Project: (Page 38), Vignettes of Light
(Page 60), A Floating Stairway
(page 104)

WESTWOODS
4747 Pearl Street
Boulder, CO 80301 USA
T: 303-449-2071
W: www.westwoods.com
Project: Vignettes of Light
(Page 60)

MANUFACTURERS, SUPPLIERS, PRODUCTS, AND ONLINE RESOURCES

Please note that all phone numbers appear as they would be dialed in the country of their origin. You will need to consult a phone book for international country codes (and in some cases, city codes) and instructions for dialing overseas. The (o) represents a zero that is included when dialing within the country, but left off when dialing that number from overseas.

ALKCO LIGHTING
11500 Melrose Avenue
Franklin Park, IL 60131 USA
T: 847-451-0700
F: 847-451-7152
W: www.alkco.com

ALLSCAPE
2930 South Fairview
Santa Ana, CA 92704 USA
T: 800-854-8277
F: 714-668-1107
W: www.alllighting.com

AMERICAN LIGHTING ASSOCIATION
T: 800-BRIGHTIDEAS
W: www.americanlightingassoc.com

AMEICO
W: www.ameico.com

ARDEE LIGHTING
639 Washburn Switch Road
P.O. Box 1769
Shelby, NC 28151 USA
T: 704-482-2811
F: 704-484-0818
W: www.ardeelighting.com

ARTEMIDE
1980 New Highway
Farmingdale, NY 11735 USA
T: 631-694-9292
F: 631-694-9482
W: www.artemide.us

BALLARD
T: 800-367-2775
W: www.ballarddesigns.com

BELFER
P.O. Box 2079
Ocean, NJ 07712 USA
T: 732-493-2666
F: 732-493-2941
W: www.belfergroup.com

BELLISSIMO
Terry Murphy
The Galleria
351 Leadville Avenue, North
Ketchum, ID 83340 USA
T: 208-726-0702
F: 208-726-0705
W: www.bellissimo-sv.com

BLANCHE FIELD
Kevin Todd
T: 617-423-0715

BULBS.COM
T: 508-363-2800
F: 508-363-2900
W: www.bulbs.com

CHERRY TREE DESIGN
320 Pronghorn Trail
Bozeman, MT 59718 USA
T: 406-582-9604
W: www.cherrytreedesign.com

CSI LIGHTING
Room 1303. No. 2088
Huiyin Building
Hudshan Road
Shanghai, 200030 China
T: 0086-21-545-10771
F: 0086-21-545-10772
W: www.cslighting.com
E: sales@cslighting.com

DELA TORRE DESIGN STUDIOS
526 West 26th Street
New York, NY 10001 USA
T: 212-243-5202
W: www.delatorredesign.com

EDISON PRICE LIGHTING
W: www.EPL.com

FAD LIGHTING
2950 N.W. 27th Street, Building 15
Fort Lauderdale, FL 33311 USA
T: 954-677-9800
F: 954-677-1007
W: www.fadlighting.com
(U.S. distributors of "Zoom" by Serien)

FAULDING ARCHITECTURE
Heather Faulding
11 East 22nd Street
New York, NY 10010 USA
T: 212-253-9172
W: www.f2inc.com

FIRE FARM LIGHTING
P. O. Box 458
104 First Street, S. W.
Elkaden, IA 52043 USA
T: 563-245-3515
W: www.firefarm.com
E: info@firefarm.com

FORECAST, A LIGHTOLIER COMPANY
1600 Fleetwood Drive
Elgin, IL 60123 USA
T: 800-234-0416
F: 847-622-1117
W: www.forecastltg.com

FORMICA
W: www.formica.com

GENERAL ELECTRIC
W: www.gelighting.com

HUBBARDTON FORGE
154 Route 30 South
Castleton, VT 05735 USA
T: 888-826-4766
www: www.vtforge.com

INTERNATIONAL ASSOCIATION OF
LIGHITNG DESIGNERS (IALD)
T: 312-527-3677
W: www.iald.org

IKEA
W: www.ikea.com

INTERMATIC INCORPORATED
Intermatic Plaza
Spring Grove, IL 60081 USA
T: 815-675-2321
W: www.intermatic.com

IVALO LIGHTING
2300 Computer Avenue, Ste i-2
Willow Grove, PA 19090 USA
T: 215-659-3302
F: 215-659-1006
W: www.ivalolighting.com

JUNO LIGHTING
1300 S. Wolf Road
Des Plaines, IL 60017 USA
T: 847-827-9880
W: www.junolighting.com

KARTELL
W: www.Kartell.it

KICHLER
7711 E. Pleasant Valley Road
P.O. Box 318010
Cleveland, OH 44131-8010 USA
T: 216-573-1000
F: 216-573-2270
W. www.kichler.com

LAM LIGHTING SYSTEMS
2930 South Fairview Street
Santa Ana, CA 92704 USA
T: 714-549-9765
F: 714-662-4515
W: www.lamlighting.com
E: lamlighting@lamlighting.com

LAMPI LAMPA
8034, de Chateaubriand
Montréal, Québec, Canada H2R 2M9
T: 514.279.5474
W: www.lampilampa.com
E: info@lampilampa.com

LAURA ASHLEY UK
P. O. Box 19
Newtown
Powys
SY16 1DZ
UK
W: www.lauraashley.com

LEUCOS USA
11 Mayfield Avenue
Edison, NJ 08837 USA
T: 732-225-0010
F: 732-225-0250
W: www.leucos.com

LIGHTLY EXPRESSED LIGHT BARS
c/o Fiberstars
44259 Nobel Drive
Freemon, CA 94538 USA
T: 800-327-7877
W: www.fiberstars.com

LITHONIA LIGHTING
P.O. Box A
Conyers, GA 30012 USA
T: 770-922-9000
F: 770-483-2635
W: www.lithonia.com

LUCIFER LIGHTING
414 Live Oak Street
San Antonio, TX 78202 USA
T: 800-879-9797
F: 210-227-4967
W: www.luciferlighting.com

LUTRON ELECTRONICS CO. INC.
Coppersburg, PA 18036 USA
T: 610-282-3800
F: 610-282-6437
W: www.lutron.com
E: product@lutron.com

METALARTE
c/o Hinson Lighting
27-35 Jackson Avenue
Long Island City, NY 11101-2917 USA
T: 718-482-1100
F: 718-937-7566

MODERN FAN COMPANY
T: 888-588-3267
W: www.modernfan.com

NESSEN
420 Railroad Way
P.O. Box 187
Mamaroneck, NY 10543-0187 USA
T: 914-698-7799
F: 914-698-5577
W: www.nessenlighting.com

NICOLETTE BRUNKLAUS
W: www.brunklaus.nl

OUTDOOR LIGHTING PERSPECTIVES
7233 Pineville Matthews Road
Charlotte, NC 28226 USA
T: 704-341-8383 or 877-898-8808
W: www.outdoorlights.com

PHILLIPS LIGHTING
W: www.nam.lighintg.phillips.com/
us/consumer

PRESCOLITE
101 Corporate Drive
Spartanburg, SC 29303 USA
T: 864-599-6000
F: 864-599-6151
W: www.prescolite.com

PROGRESS LIGHTING
P.O. Box 5704
Spartanburg, SC 29304-5704 USA
T: 864-699-1332
W: www.progresslighting.com

REJUVENATION
2550 NW Nicolai Street
Portland, OR 97210 USA
T: 888-401-1900
W: www.rejuvenation.com

RESTORATION HARDWARE
104 Challenger Drive
Portland, TN 37148-1703 USA
T: 800-762-1005
W: www.restorationhardware.com

ROCKSCAPES
9185 Kelvin Avenue
Chatsworth, CA 91311 USA
T: 800-677-6811
F: 818-882-7136
W: www.rsllighting.com
E: sales@rsllighting.com

ROTALIANA
15 Old Sherman Turnpike
Danbury, CT 06810 USA
T: 800-713-2182
F: 800-713-2481
W: www.nalights.com

or

ELETTRICA ROTALIANA SRL
Via della rupe 35
38017 Mezzolombardo
(trento) Italy
C.F. e P.IVA 01236060222
T: +39 0461-602376
F: +39-0461-602-539
W: www.rotaliana.it
E: info@rotaliana.it

RSL
1075 Indian Head Industrial Blvd.
St. Louis, MO 63132 USA
T: 314-429-5483
F: 314-429-5489
W: www.rsl-lite.com

SCALA
c/o Luxo Corporation
200 Clearbrook Road
Elmsford, NY 10523 USA
T: 914-345-0067
F: 914-345-0068
W: www.luxous.com

SCHOOLHOUSE ELECTRIC
330 Southeast Martin Luther King Jr.
Boulevard
Portland, OR 97214 USA
T: 503-230-7113
F: 503-230-7082
W: www.schoolhouseelecric.com

SERIEN
Raumleuchten GmbH
Hainhäuser Str. 3-7
D-63110 Rodgau
T: (0 61 06) 69 09-0
F: (0 61 06) 69 09-22
W: www.serien.com
("Zoom" distributed in U.S. by FAD
Lighting)

SHADY LADY LIGHTING
1350 14th Avenue, Suite 14
Grafton, WI 53024 USA
T: 262-377-6848 or 800-343-1954
F: 262-377-7190
W: www.shadyladylighting.com
E: info@shadyladylighting.com

SOLUTUBE INTERNATIONAL
T: 800-966-7652
W: www.solatube.com

STARFIRE LIGHTING
7 Donna Drive
Woodbridge, NJ 07075 USA
T: 800-443-8823
F: 201-438-9541
W: www.starfirelighting.com
E: info@starfirelighting.com

STERNBERG OUTDOOR LIGHTING
555 Lawrence Ave
Roselle, IL 60172 USA
T: 847-588-3400
F: 847-588-3440
W: www.sternberglighting.com

SUPER BRIGHT LEDS
St. Louis, MO, 63031 USA
T: 314-972-6200
W: www.superbrightleds.com

TECH LIGHTING
7400 Linder Avenue
Skokie, IL 60077 USA
T: 847-410-4400
F: 847-410-4500
W: www.techlighting.com
Email: sales_support@techlighting.com

TRESCO INTERNATIONAL
801 E. Middletown Rd.
North Lima, OH 44452 USA
T: 800-227-1171 or 330-549-2230
F: 800-841-2523 or 330-549-2260
W: www.trescointernational.com
E: custsvc@trescointl.com

URBAN ARCHEAOLOGY
143 Franklin Street
New York, NY 10013 USA
T: 212-431-4646
W: www.urbanarcheology.com

W.A.C. LIGHTING
615 South Street
Garden City, NY 11530 USA
T: 800-526-2588 or 516-515-5000
W: www.waclighting.com/USA
E: sales@waclighting.com/USA

WALO BERTSCHINGER AG
Giessenstrasse 5
8952 Schlieren
T: +41 1 745 23 11
W: www.walo.ch/

ZANEEN LIGHTING
65 Densley Avenue
Toronto, Ontario, Canada, M6M 2P5
T: 416-247-9221 or 800-388-3382
F: 416-247-9319
W: www.zaneen.com

PHOTOGRAPHER CREDITS

Dennis Anderson/Randall Whitehead Lighting, Inc., 5 (top left & right; bottom, left); 7 (middle, top); 7 (bottom); 92; 93; 96; 97; 111; 140; 141; 142; 143; 144; 145

Marc Cramer, 68; 69

DMAC Architecture, P.C., Dwayne MacEwen, Principal, 98; 100; 101; 107

Elliott + Associates Architects/Robert Shimer, Hedrich Blessing, 6 (middle & bottom); 7 (middle, bottom); 36; 72; 73; 74; 75; 151; 152; 154; 155

Jason S. Gray/Kanner Architects, 133

Sam Gray, 7 (top); 94

George Gruel/www.oddstick.com, 6 (middle, bottom); 13; 105; 114; 115; 116; 117; 118; 119

Pernilla Hed, 109

Bruno Helbling/zapaimages, 7 (middle); 54 (left); 55; 113; 146; 147; 148; 149

Douglas Hope Hooper/Avalon Artistic Landscape Lighting, 122; 123; 124; 125; 128; 129; 130; 131

John Edward Linden, 126; 127

David Ling, Architect, 56; 57; 78; 79

Deborah Whitlaw Llewellyn, 89

Mark Luscombe-White/The Interior Archive, 5 (middle, right); 66; 67

Björg Magnea, 47; 48; 49; 58; 59; 76; 77; 90; 91; 135; 136; 137; 138; 139

Ray Main/www.mainstreamimages.co.uk, 71; 86; 87; 162; 163; 164; 165; 166; 167

Nacasa & Partners, Inc., 156, 157, 158, 159, 160, 161

Eric Roth, 8; 50; 51; 52; 53; 65; 85; 103; 106

Courtesy of Schoolhouse Electric Co., 5 (bottom, right); 10

Richard Sexton, 40; 41; 43; 45; 80; 81; 82; 83

Tarlton Studios/Ron Yeo, Architect, 120; 121

Courtesy of Tech Lighting, 5 (middle, left)

Verbeck Design Studios, Inc., 6 (top; middle, top); 39; 61; 62; 63; 104

ACKNOWLEDGMENTS

I would like to thank the wonderfully talented architects, designers, and lighting designers I had the honor of working with. Your knowledge and insights are invaluable to not only this book, but to the entire industry. I am also indebted to the gracious manufacturers of lighting fixtures and lamps that helped this book come alive. I want to extend a special thank you to Rockport Publisher Winnie Prentiss, graphics coordinator Cora Hawks, and especially Betsy Gammons, who in my book will always be the #1 photo editor and project manager an author could ever have. Betsy's never-ending patience, tireless diplomacy, sure attention to detail, and irreplaceable relationships with photographers will always be respected by many, including this author. Last, but never least, I'd like to thank Steve, Chloe, and Connor for understanding the long hours I spend chained to my computer.

ABOUT THE AUTHOR

Interior design and architectural writer and editor Marilyn Zelinsky-Syarto is also the author of *The Inspired Workspace* (Rockport Publishers, 2002), *New Workplaces for New Workstyles* (McGraw Hill, 1998), *Practical Home Office Solutions* (McGraw Hill, 1999) and contributing author to *Pottery Barn Home* (Oxmoor House, 2005). She has also written for several distinguished design magazines including *Interiors*, *ASID Icon*, and *Woman's Day Special Interest Publications*. A former editor at Taunton Press, she has also edited a number of highly regarded architecture and design books. She and her family live in Fairfield, Connecticut.